When Time and Space Conspire

When Time and Space Conspire

An Anthology Celebrating Twenty-Five Years of the Austin International Poetry Festival

Edited by

Dr. Charles A. Stone and Becky Liestman

Volume 07
Written Word Series
RHR Leaning Tree Adventures Inc.

The poetry in this volume is the original work of the poets who have granted one-time publication rights to LTA. All rights reserved. No part of this book may be reproduced or transmitted in any form or by any means (electronic, mechanical, magnetic, photographic, photocopy, recording, and any other storage or retrieval system) without prior written permission of the publisher and author. No patent liability is assumed with respect to the use of the information contained herein. Although every precaution has been taken in the preparation of this book, the publisher and author assume no responsibility for errors or omissions. Neither is any liability assumed for damages resulting from the use the information contained herein.

COPYRIGHT © 2017 by RHR Leaning Tree Adventures

ISBN 978-1539650997

RHR Leaning Tree Adventures Inc.
3518 Clairmont, San Antonio, TX 78259

When Time and Space Conspire

An Anthology Celebrating Twenty-Five Years of the Austin International Poetry Festival

Participating Poets

Christine Beck
June Blumenson
Lynn Wheeler Brandstetter
Claire Vogel Camargo
Barbara Crooker
Charles Darnell
Patricia Dixon
Shelley Getten
Joyce Gullickson
Mike Gullickson
Jonathan Harrington
Hemmingplay
Angela Hunt
Gilbert Juergens III
Glynn Monroe Irby
A. Marie Kaluza
Becky Liestman
John Looker
Mia Loweree

Aimee Mackocic
Neil Meili
Sharon Meixsell
John Milkereit
Jeffrey Morgan
Marsh Muirhead
James B. Nicola
Nuart (Nvard Chalikyan)
David Orchard
Jim Parker
Georg Reilly
Paul Richmond
Brian Smith
Patricia Young Smith
Dr. Charles A. Stone
Susan Summers
Joyce Sutphen
Michele Vecchitto
Roger West

Table of Contents

This Poem	1
Equinox	2
Phases	3
The Irrational Numbers of Longing…	4
At the Last Chance Saloon	4
Sometimes I Am Startled Out of Myself	5
As Time Always Does	6
Defying Gravity	7
Transmigration	8
E-Mail from a Small Star	9
Goddess of the First Hour	10
A Dream of the Future	11
The Posthumous Journey of the Soul	12
A Postcard from the Barren	13
The Blue Eternity	14
The Going Back	15
There Are Multiple Versions of You	16
Washing Machine	17
Physics and Poetry Collide	18
The Arc of Time	19
I Open My Life	20
The Future of Music	21
Steven Hawking Says Don't Phone Back	22
The Insomniac's Guide to Oblivion	23
The Mayor's Guide to Reelection	23
The Insomniac's Guide to Reciprocity	24
Raiding the Deep	25
Bottom Remembers Love	26
In the Time of El Dorado	27
First Landfall in Nova Scotia	28
The Arrival	29
Violin (1778)	30
Frequent Flyers	30
Disclaimers on Reading	32
Before I Start Reading This	33
The Mudslingers	34
Enter My Honeycombed Vault	35
If We Lived at Sarah Oppenheimer's *D-17*	36

Latitudes and Attitudes	37
Déjà Vu	38
Keeper of the Fields	40
Dream Receiver	42
Bitter Truths	43
Gratitude	44
Our Time	45
Entre Deux Souffles	46
Between Two Breaths	47
Camera Obscura	48
Someone and Me	49
Whatever Must Come Down, Comes Down Without…	50
Normandy	50
Feeding Chickens	51
For Clarity's Sake	52
After Reading Translations of Love	52
Hiking the Universe	53
A Tribute to Our Favorite Spot	54
April 21, 2016	55
Dare	56
Tattoos and Scars	57
Purple Vespers	58
Self Portrait as Gigi, Favorite Childhood Doll	59
Requiem for a Kiss	60
Preincarnated	61
The Gift of Pottery	62
Molcajete	62
Awakened Man	64
Vapor	65
Easel	65
Surprising, Isn't It?	66
Pre-retirement Mail	67
Riverstone Words	68
Adrift	69
Listening to Stones	70
Wilderness	71
Turning Sixty	72
Questions About Glass	73
The Fallen	75
Still Life	76

What It's All About	77
Life Beginning	78
Revenir	79
When Death Prevails	80
Night Skies	81
Unpacking for the Trip	82
Have You Ever Woken	83
The Wrong Place	84
Friends Strangers Multitudes	85
Traces	86
Quantum Lunch	87
Rule Britannica	87
Dante's 9th Inning Stretch	88
Ode to NASA	89
Simplicity	90
Fout-Ta-Ta-Rou	91
Because the Bible Tells Me So	92
Throughout the Long Night	93
In Hospice	94
Haunting	95
Who We Are	96
Songs of Newborns	97
Beyond the Door	98
Phosphor Nights	99
The Swan Goose	99
Jump-Fly Journeys	102
Imagi 06	103
Timeless Travel	104
Celestial Plan	105
Mist of Time	106
More than Dreams	107
Generation XO	108
Trapped in Time	109
The Buoyancy of Light	110
The Tunes of Life	111
Birds Make Holes in Heaven	112
North of Tombstone, 3 AM	112
All Is Temporary	114
Breathe Briefly	115
The Mystery of the Universe	116

Be There (Between My Sun and My Clouds)	117
The Truthful Mirror	118
Your Name	119
Nature Boy	120
Galactic Star Child	121
Sleep	122
It's Raining Leaves	123
Beyond and Before Time and Space	124
Inside the Sun	125
A Drop in the Ocean of Space	127
Stanley Was Waving	128
She Already Knew	129
I Have Some Questions	130
Referents	133
Unsung Melodies of Sisterhood	134
Dreams of a Poet	135
The Quaint Angel	136
In the Gaps	137
Palacios, TX and the Universe	138
Edge of Madness	139
Seeing Infinity	140
Illusion of Time	141
A Poet's Box of Time	142
String Theory	144
The Impossible Logic of Time	145
Time Traveler: For My Son	146
The Excellent Now	147
Visions, Dreams	148
The World Spins	149
Flight Delay	150
The Missing	151
Memory Care	152
October moon (first line)	153
three a.m. (first line)	153
I can't see you now (first line)	153
longest night of the year (first line)	153
last week of school (first line)	153
last night of the carnival (first line)	153
a thousand snows (first line)	153
Wrong Train	154

A Bedridden Lullaby	155
Upon Some Other Shore	156
Slow	157
Gray Running	159
Voodoo in Cartagena	160
Memoir	161
A Dog's Life	162
You Don't Have to Be a House to Be Haunted	163
Ancestral Dream	164
Stuff of Wounds	165
Given Salt, Given Time	166
I am Writing to You from the End of the World	167
Time Sensitive Material	168
Rewind	169
Grand Mound: A Sacred Prehistoric Site…	171
Kay, One More Time	172
Meditation	173
My First Pocket	174
Hear Me	175
She Did Not Hear	176
Specimens Like Us	177
China 1013 A.D.	178
Hey, I Say	179
On My Doorstep, I Expect a Miracle	180
In the Creases	181
The Easy Bridge	182
Spheres of Reality	183
Medicine Wheel	184
Chance Encounter	185
Unfamiliar Form	186
Parallel Lives	187
Everywhere the Stars	188
Publication Credits	189
Biographical Sketches	196

Preface

We think of poets as collectors. Imagine walking along a serene beach, picking up flotsam and jetsam, putting it all into a beach bucket. Something interesting is found, followed by something else that is perhaps more interesting. Throughout the day, it becomes obvious that some items, like broken shells, are easy to find, while it is difficult to find other things, like old arrowheads.

A collector must be in the right place at the right time to make significant discoveries. To put it another way, a collector must *become* the beach in order to see what isn't readily apparent. That's poetry: finding what is exactly right, even if it's hidden among the detritus on the beach, in literature, or in the space that surrounds us!

As poets, we're always searching for words, paring them down and honing them, attempting to capture those with just the right shade of meaning. As we attempt to discover what is hidden, we sometimes surprise ourselves with the brilliance of illumination, the way discovery takes unexpected turns, deep into truth.

This anthology, *When Time and Space Conspire*, leads us high into the stars and outer-worlds, into the hinterlands of the spirit, and back and forth through time. What better landscape to collect poetic ideas than the vast reaches of the galaxies, sorting the extraordinary from the ordinary, looking at the shifting planet earth, or seeing the intimate touch of a blue-veined hand explore the terrain between life and death. In the poems that follow, parallel universes, multiple dimensions of human experience and apparent shifts in frames of time reflect the complexities of life, and sometimes, it's simplicity.

We are delighted to offer the poems in this diverse anthology. They are drawn from poets across the U.S. and foreign locales. They are the voices of very accomplished, nationally known poets, and those who are new to the craft. Each of the poets is a dedicated collector of thoughts. Thank you for hearing their voices.

Barbara Crooker

This Poem

is a clothesline hanging
between two trees;
the words, hung by wooden
pegs, move with the wind.
Between the lines, punctuations
of iris, peonies, bleeding hearts,
and a meadow that stretches
as far as the pines. It has been raining
all night. Someone I once loved
appears in the margins; I no longer
remember his name. The wind roams
through the trees, and two crows
resume their argument, not caring
anymore who's wrong, who's right,
make inky tracks across the page.
The fog of memory blurs the text,
words running wild in the field.
I hear horns blowing, as the boat
comes into the harbor, my grandmother,
a small girl, looking over the rail
as the new world rises before her.
I smell steam rising from ironed cotton
as my mother slicks down the sheets.
The blank pages flap in the breeze.
What else can this poem contain,
except the world, and everything in it?

Barbara Crooker

Equinox

Another October. The maples have done their slick trick
of turning yellow almost overnight; summer's hazy skies
are cobalt blue. My friend has come in from the West,
where it's been a year of no mercy: chemotherapy, bone
marrow transplant, more chemotherapy, and her hair
came out in fistfuls, twice. Bald as a pumpkin.
And then, the surgeon's knife.
But she's come through it all, annealed by fire,
calm settled in her bones like the morning mist in valleys
and low places, and her hair's returned, glossy
as a horse chestnut kept in a shirt pocket.
Today a red fox ran down through the corn stubble;
he vanished like smoke. I want to praise things
that cannot last. The scarlet and orange leaves
are already gone, blown down by a cold rain,
crushed and trampled. They rise again in leaf meal
and wood smoke. The Great Blue Heron's returned to the pond,
settles in the reeds like a steady flame.
Geese cut a wedge out of the sky, drag the gray days
behind them like a skein of old wool.
I want to praise everything brief and finite.
Overhead, the Pleiades fall into place; Orion rises.
Great Horned Owls muffle the night with their calls;
night falls swiftly, tucking us in her black velvet robe,
the stitches showing through, all those little lights,
our little lives, rising and falling.

Barbara Crooker

Phases

It's the moon, isn't it, that calls you
all your life, menarche to menopause,
pregnancy to blank black sky, the dark
night when there is no light, anywhere.
Sometimes, I see my grandmother's face
when it's round and full, the crevasses
and craters that mark the surface.
Sometimes, when it goes gibbous,
I see my mother, as her light fades
and dims. Waxing or waning,
I think of my daughters, the oldest
just joining the circle of women
with the birth of her first, the youngest
still finding her rhythm in the great
dance. But what calls me most often
in the still night sky are the crescents,
slim fingernail parings, tiny commas
of light, perhaps undreamed granddaughters,
or some other future, but always that beacon,
that shine in the sky that will bloom
into a lamp, throw light on everything
that dances under its glimmer.

Barbara Crooker

The Irrational Numbers of Longing, The Infinite Mathematics of Desire

This day could be reduced to three elements:
green grass, blue hills, yellow fields of mustard,
solid in its planes as any late Cézanne. It makes me think
of the curves your hips and back make when you are sleeping,
the way my fingers travel the back road of your spine,
the landscape of our bodies under the quilt.

I want to relearn the language of plane geometry,
the relationship of curves in space, the friction
between positive and negative numbers, improper
fractions, your lovely smooth surface, the angle
of intersection, where we come together in the dark.

At the Last Chance Saloon

The moon's a half dollar tossed on the bar,
somebody's loose change. The cold gin in the Dipper
shimmers. We seem to think we can spend it all,
that our resources will endlessly replenish, as profligate
as stars in the sky's deep pocket. But the ice caps
are melting, the permafrost is thawed, oil reserves
sucked dry, while we turn our backs on energy
harvested from sun and wind. No winners
here. Pile on the down quilts. The days grow shorter.
Turn up the thermostat, open the window. Now,
while we've got it, let everything burn.

Barbara Crooker

Sometimes, I Am Startled Out of Myself

like this morning, when the wild geese came squawking,
flapping their rusty hinges, and something about their trek
across the sky made me think about my like, the places
of brokenness, the places of sorrow, the places where grief
has strung me out to dry. And then the geese come calling,
the leader falling back when tired, another taking her place.
Hope is borne on wings. Look at the trees. They turn to gold
for a brief while, then lose it all each November.
Through the cold months, they stand, take the worst
weather has to offer. And still, they put out shy green leaves
come April, come May. The geese glide over the cornfields,
land on the pond with it sedges and reeds.
You do not have to be wise. Even a goose knows how to find
shelter, where the corn still lies in the stubble and dried stalks.
All we do is pass through here, the best way we can.
They stitch up the sky, and it is whole again.

Joyce Sutphen

As Time Always Does

Everything was changing; nothing was.
The road that used to be gravel was tarred.
We watched, and time did as time always does.

It put houses in the fields, and across
the woods it made an ugly cut; it scarred
everything with progress. Nothing was

safe from the crowbar and the ripsaw's buzz.
Time carried a hammer and hammered hard
as we watched. It did what it always does.

It wanted things: stores and movies, new laws
that said you had to have a neat green yard.
Everything was changing. Nothing was

left of the old quiet that wrapped like gauze
around the wound each minute made. On guard,
we watched, and time did as time always does.

Someday no one will remember us;
the sky will be as now, remotely starred.
Everything was changing; nothing was.
We watched while time did as time always does.

Joyce Sutphen

Defying Gravity

Sometimes I think you must be
the man in the moon,
holding your little dog in your arms,
looking kindly towards the blue marble
of your birth, covering the walls of
the universe with drawings of
motorcycles and lost boys.

Or I think you must be
a cosmic pilgrim, with your
invisible staff and the magic
beans you traded for one of our
cows so that you could climb
a ladder into the sky
and ride in a giant's hat,

but sometimes I think you're still
the kid who doesn't want to go
to school. There I am, trying to talk
you into going inside, telling you
how much fun you'll have,
and there you are, flying
from one tree to another like a bird.

Joyce Sutphen

Transmigration

It will happen when the soul is ready
to leave the body at last. I suppose
there will be something in the way the light
falls, or the stars themselves will point the way.

Like birds we will gather as summer ends,
ready to mount the flyway our mothers
told us about long ago. We know there
will be a place for us when we arrive.

Whether or not this will happen again
is not clear. We often have the feeling
that we have been in these places before,
but for now it's only a matter of

waiting quietly for the wind to rise
and going along wherever it goes.

Joyce Sutphen

E-mail from a Small Star

I am light years away
but I would like you to know
that I was shining for you
fifty thousand years before
you arrived on earth.

I am expecting great things
of you because I can see
the future and the past –
both at the same time.
Your life is a good story,

When I sing your song
across the deserts of space
and into the deep tunnels
of lost time, I tell them
how hard it was to be alive.

Bodies, I say, were only
a temporary innovation,
as were all those choices
you had to make about
good and evil. Good won

in the end – I thought you
would like to know that.
The place where you are now
eventually becomes heaven.

After a while, no one ever
dies, and everyone understands
each other. It's quite amazing.
I thought you'd like to know.

Joyce Sutphen

Goddess of the First Hour

As soon as there was time,
there was change.

If I did not remember you,
the sky would collapse;

everything I touch would fall
to pieces; even the stars

would leave their constellations;
the sky would be darker than night.

The world, as we know it,
requires an end –

a truth that has acquired
its beauty along the way.

Joyce Sutphen

A Dream of the Future

The future that never happens
is the one that makes us do
what we do while we are waiting
for what is never going to come
and take us away from the past,
which is a country that we do not
know anymore, where the language
is strange, only almost familiar.

Years not only go by, they carry us
into places where we meet the dragons,
the gorgons, the pack of wolves
circling with their sharp teeth, and
sometimes we lift a candle, sometimes curse.
Like scarecrows, we scare a bird or two.
We know what we are and are not.

But still we keep on dreaming, warming
our hands over the fire in that cottage
at the end of the road – where everything
is prepared for us, and someone we
never met has departed only minutes ago.

Joyce Sutphen

The Posthumous Journey of the Soul

What to bring along? Nothing.
Everything. Even the smallest rock
is too heavy to lift, and whether
you can carry even a bird's song
in your ear is uncertain.

And where to go? Not back along
those roads you knew when you
were living in the body – not even
into the dreams that came at night –
but somewhere out there, beyond
anything you have imagined.

There are some things you will recognize:
a palm tree beyond the last thought,
a thing with feathers that perches in the soul,
and a woman, lovely in her bones.
Once you pass the gate, it will be only
you . . . and the windy sky.

Joyce Sutphen

A Postcard from the Burren

The quarry down the hill is deep,
its walls no different
than those of the ruined houses

we pass when we go to find
the horses, doorways gaped open,
dirt floors, the view going through

to the hillside where bushes
still yield berries, sweet
purples in the long green grass.

We do not know who lived there,
the sound of them is so long gone
their echo is past Jupiter.

Becky Liestman

The Blue Eternity

Call it the ocean, the deep
Call it life
Call it death
A changeling, it morphs –
A wet force spreading and evaporating

Brave blue water
Volatile…Wonderful
A Paleolithic presence repeated over the globe
Across magnificent innumerable galaxies
Water that was – is
Or certainly will be

Somewhere
Life exists --

For the possible *others*, in the far reaches of outer space
Who are clearly and certainly not us;
For our billions of human cells, heavy with it, fostering each life
For an ordinary spill, trickling through my fingers…There it goes…

Drop, Drip

Becky Liestman

The Going Back

Wandering about in yourself
wondering if you'll get somewhere in that cranky
old closet, closed up and mothballed.
Perhaps you'll find your intention
or some life instruction,
perhaps a maze of images
you didn't try to hang on to forever –
like clothes on a far off clothesline
lit by unexpected tripwires
a lightning bolt or the aurora borealis rushing
a living color across your brow.
The stray paths you wander in your mental wheelchair
become a destination. Done with forwards
you move backwards. In afterthought
the road behind is always thirsty.
Swallow before you drink.

There Are Multiple Versions of You?

Out there in parallel universes
a lot is happening. Perhaps.
Physicists use algorithms and experiments
to confirm mathematical abstractions.
They explore theories. They probe. They verify.
They design rigorous trials in labs to see
a single electron move, and stand still, at the same time.
When we're not dreaming of TV
or gaming Apps or making tonight's
dinner, when we're content and thoughtful –
for these moments we might take a mental journey
into quantum mechanics, where simultaneous
events occur in the fabric of spacetime. What if each
choice you make branches out, creating another you? Or if past
events are happening now? Reality may purposefully
confine us, waiting patiently for our limited vision to expand.

Becky Liestman

Washing Machine

You are right, all the time. Spin
the clothes, make them clean.
You see the world in cycles.
Cleanliness next to Godliness.
Have you given any thought
to the meaning of dirt?
The vast soils that cover
the earth? Can they really
be erased? It's the repetition
that gets me going. Round and round.
It's the implosion of the grand *us*
(deceit, *la guerre*, illogic)
merged with bad water and too much spin.
I've been expecting static, stasis
the clothes folded and placed in
pairs of drawers. Neat and wholesome
for eternity. What was I thinking?

Becky Liestman

Physics and Poetry Collide

Sparse l e t t e
        Rs
    On a page   rumMors code? eBook?

Less **more** than more   *itself*?

Make lines   who can't look back, see how they

run

So trite

     Maybe add

Factors of 3, multipliers by the doz'in,   oops……dozen?

(It's combination confusing)
          a trail of words in form ula?

      Math sestinas?

   faster,
glance away—

    till connections appear

        More like vast threads of yarn, scattered.

A parallel of sorts. UNRAVELING

                   Waitin' for the quantum muse

Look elsewhere or

she's gone.

The Arc of Time

Peer into an electron microscope.
That's the time my uncle has to see the invisible,
to type articles and papers
on his old typewriter before the computer world
explodes...
A switch to keyboards is easy.
His thoughts are important. Get them in print.
Conferences across the world read messages
in the night sky, and delve into the unseeable. I search
quietly for me, in kindergarten. Big and small reflect.

Discovery is constant. Belief
is endless. He brings me a small, wired
doll in peasant cloth (from France) which could
possibly be the moon. He's goes to far flung
places, asking big questions. He's irritated, intrigued,
but mainly obsessed. No clear answers.
I wrestle ideas. And social cues. I learn to consider
carefully as I grow into this bold galaxy.
But the skin on my hands soon grows loose
and shows off my blue veins.

Becky Liestman

I Open My Life

The sun rises on my igoogle
page and bits made into sand
glow
streaming sunrise and sunset
to my emails in gmail.

This is my home
page where top stories   reside
and I can add stuff.
The sun in full bloom right now

why not edit, delete, share

my account (ing) of this life?
My facebook is twittering a dance of topics-
I switch back to classic home
before I sign   out.

A good idea?
(Ruminating) I make mac and cheese
the old-fashioned way on a burner
bright with red   heat.

Calm down, I tell it.
Like me, it never listens
except to the smear of turquoise waves,
and the sunset, sunrise   painted on ceramic tile
just above my   stove.

Life. I'd type my tale but my keyboard hesitates.
I politely ask what password it requires
to bring me to the table.

The Future of Music

When the band plays
Strikes at our senses in the darkened
Space   the night-lights dim
I feel transported
Big noise bends my hearing
I grasp notes, stilted sound
and night-lights dim
All the machines in the world
Pound computer dance rhythms
My toes tap
The floor is metallic
My toes tap
I feel the lift-off
Wavery, sublime
Difficult to fathom at first
Night-lights flicker, the tempo builds
I go still in my chair
The robots punch buttons
To my left, to my right
Sensors sparkle
The band plays
On, we are off
Into the stars
I am here, one of many
What a way to depart

Becky Liestman

Steven Hawking Says Don't Answer Back

If aliens call, don't expect to live at the top
of the food chain.
This is not survivor TV. If they appear
I won't have my way with them –

After all, they're not the boys in junior high
easy to tease and confuse.
Not my parents calling "Don't slam that door"
which I can respond to or not
depending on the punishment
I'm willing to take.
Not the teenagers at White Castle
on a Friday night who slouch by their cars
in the parking lot
aiming to disturb anyone they can
in some way or another.
And certainly not the metallic disembodied voices
on the police radio, surrounded by static
in squad cars resembling unmarked tanks –

Don't answer their alien phone.
We beamed Morse Code years ago
begging for a visit, too late to withdraw
the invitation now. Near space is filled
with our signals. On the flip side, hiding
is a good strategy. Let's blanket
our airwaves, rein in our spacecraft,
and go to bed in camouflage.

The Insomniac's Guide to Oblivion

Maybe the space between memories is excessively beautiful
like the space between people you love
who will never move any closer to each other.
Let's call this the universe, and say it fills the room at night.
You see things that are not there
next to things that are. This is how we feel
about the dead in old pictures
where their clothes are all wrong. We wonder
how long until we are born.

The Mayor's Guide to Reelection

Notice how reflections stutter along a bank of windows,
into and out of the spaces between them
like a choppy reel of film. It is your job to imagine
how a man changes, how he becomes his doppelgangers.
To be local is to halve a distance
an infinite number of times. In the sunlight of early autumn
and among long shadows of old buildings,
reminiscent of deadfalls, you can hear
several versions of a myth about perseverance.
Every time you forget someone's name, a child falls in a field.
No one can teach you how to move towards another
to embrace before leaving, or how to get so close
without touching. No one remembers
who found the first child in a field and carried her home.

Jeffrey Morgan

The Insomniac's Guide to Reciprocity

Strike a match to hear the hole it tears in the night:
your very own tiny parenthesis.

Let that drip of heat fall towards your fingers
until you remember how soft nothing can be.

Strike another. This is the law of diminishing returns.
This is why fire is not the opposite of emptiness,

and why you are not growing younger
no matter how many times you sign your name this way.

The air that is all around you is also on the other side
of the world. You dig down with the same mind

you have always had, knowing only more,
and with something less and less like surprise each time

 the burn follows you into the dark.

John Looker

Raiding the Deep

Let's spin the globe, spin it towards the sun –
slowly now – we're looking for a likely place,
a place where the sea or the ocean touch the land
and men have always put to sea in boats,
have moored their boats or dragged them on the shore
with heavy limbs after the homeward run.

Here will do,
here where the wild Atlantic batters the coast
and the heaving tide has carried a fragile fleet
up on to Portugal's sand. The boats are beached
and the sardine catch laid out in boxes for the buyers,
and men with wide-brimmed metal hats
will carry the fish on their heads, salt water dripping,
up to the trucks and out of view.

Soon the men will hear how much they've earned.
A decent trip? Not bad.
The catch? So-so.
Not as much as in the glory days
but the weather held, the fish were there, the gear behaved
and (although this isn't said) they all returned.

Spin the world,
and find the trawlers active in early morning
off Newfoundland, Nova Scotia and New England.
Spin it and in the darkness look for vessels
ranged around the Pacific ring of fish,

tuned to their weather warnings, studying sonar,
watching the stars in shoals expiring slowly
and the depths putting on new colour,
as the day – a day of promise –
is unfurled.

John Looker

Bottom Remembers Love

All them years ago but still each day
she's flitting in and out of my dreams ... her eyes
like pools at night full of the moon and stars,
her smile pure sunlight waking in the east.
She smelt of summer meadows, and when she spoke
her voice, soft and fierce, flew like an owl
hunting. I tell you I froze, while the hairs on my head
stood up, and they (you know what I mean?) weren't all.
You're right of course, they laughed and called me an ass.
Me and her, we come from different lives,
like trees that were stood on opposite banks of a river
leaning, weaving our branches, blossom, leaves.
        What could we be to each other? She were the rain
        falling on wheat ... and me warm air lifting the lark.

John Looker

In the Time of El Dorado

Beneath his feet the raft is rocking slowly.
Disdaining the cold, he stands proud
To receive the gift of the sun as it clears the peaks.

Moments before – naked, erect –
He had stood on the shore with the dark water lapping
While they clothed him in flakes of gold.

When they come to the spot of auspicious co-ordinates
He must fill his lungs and plunge
To the depths of the lake where the old gods are sleeping.

He will rise in pain, to be lifted out
With acclamation and carried to the strand with singing,
Shimmering with pearls of clear water.

Far to the east, above the undreamed-of ocean,
The sun blazes on painted ships,
Stealing forward, aching with empty holds.

John Looker

First Landfall in Nova Scotia

This was no earthly paradise
they must have thought grimly,
pressing against the gunwale
in their unwashed clothes,
lifting the smaller children
to get a better view.
They saw that they had sailed
under a chilling delusion,
bidding farewell to the land
they had known for generations.

Behind them lay the terrors
of the great Atlantic crossing:
the storms, the head-wind,
eleven weeks at sea –
each family boxed in
with its square of bare boards
allotted below decks –
food dwindling, the shared
obscenity of dysentery,
the infant deaths.

Where was the promised soil
yearning for the plough?
The pasture? No homes
waiting them, not even shelter.
Nothing but tangled forest
crowding the shore – that and
the eyes of native people,
their woodsmoke, their footprints;
all that and the wail of a bird
on a lake and autumn fading.

They sat in the forest and wept.
Then some trekked on inland
by unenticing trails. Others
stayed – gathering shellfish,
shooting moose; determined.
It was enough. Clearing trees
they constructed makeshift cabins.
Snow soon mastered all,
until at last the sun
returned – and Spring crept in.

The Arrival

"Doors to manual"
and the flight finally
lands.
We burst from the plane
like a can of cola
unzipped. At last!

All night long
in that shaken tube,
that intimate kaleidoscope
of strangers – but now
it's Passports, Baggage
and escape.

There's barely time
to drop the cases
before a child
has flown like a bird
to perch in your arms
by your cheek.

John Looker

Violin (1778)

At the height of the rebellion of His Majesty's thirteen colonies,
while the *Resolution* was charting the unknown Pacific,
Jacob Ford, master craftsman, St Paul's Churchyard London,
made this violin
and when it was complete
there he sat among the wood shavings, tools and pots of varnish
carefully tightening the strings
to set free its sweet young voice for time and the world to hear.

We look at it now and admire as he did then
its curves and glossy skin
and we lean into its song. Not long ago the bridge had broken
but that was easily fixed. Now there's a hint of a crack,
merely a hint, in the wooden panel behind.
That too could be repaired; it isn't the end.
Meanwhile the voice still sings
and Jacob Ford's gift to the world beguiles for another year.

Frequent Flyers

Camels crossing the desert in a melancholy line
stepping to Timbuktu ...

... junks of the Middle Kingdom coasting alone
and low in the water with porcelain, silks and tea ...

... tributaries

John Looker

trekking in the thin air of the Andes ...

... resolute Polynesian fleet ...
but today ... today ... we have flight.

In business class
the seats are deep and no one is too close.
From time to time they turn away
from their spreadsheets, reports and mail
or five-course airline meal
suddenly aware
of the shining clouds below:
drifting as desert sands
or tumbling like the sea's rough billows –
a sight to die for,
seen daily.
When the clouds clear,
the dream of ten thousand years
is theirs, is theirs.
                        Far below them ...

... turquoise waters of the Caribbean
and a great ray gliding, ancient, alien ...

... mile upon mile, acre on acre,
of flayed Australian ochre ...

... green meadows,
grey conurbations ...

... and a moonlit Siberia, its lakes and rivers
drawn in charcoal on a ground of silver ...

They fly on. Glass in hand
                they fly on.

John Milkereit

Disclaimers on Reading

Good evening,
I need a glass of water.
Sorry that I'm late.
Where is the microphone?
The traffic is horrible and did you know
twenty-three alcohol-related deaths have occurred
near this intersection in the past 2 weeks?
I was not informed there would be a duct-taped
brass-plated, music stand instead of a podium.
Why is there a dartboard behind my head?
I never received notification of the five-minute time
allotment of the re-enforcement with flash card
warnings and hand-waving SOS signals.
Why not turn off the televisions so no one can watch
"Monday Night Football?"
I am hallucinating from antibiotics and had planned
to arrive with 24-font bold until my printer died.
Why does the waitress continue to clang the plates
and clink the beer glasses?
I would rather eat dinner now, have a decent night of sleep,
or walk next door and fantasize over the breath-of-fire
yoga position.
But there is not enough time,
                my budget has been obliterated.
The chances of having my requests fulfilled are hopeless.
Every cost estimate of repairing my situation is at least
50% more than the cost of starting over again.
The risk of lung cancer is beyond my control,
so due to ongoing environmental concerns,
I must vacate the premises
once the cigarette smoke clears
and I see the exit sign near the mounted
deer antlers.
                                  Thank you.

John Milkereit

Before I Start Reading This

You should know words connected here
form a sort of surprise.

Not to say too much, but a sideways
Mount Kilimanajaro is revealed on the page
in a high altitude way I hope you'll enjoy.
It's what the known is blowing in your face.

For what you don't know, I brought a boom box.
The second stanza is a humpback whale recorded
from a satellite over the Indian Ocean. Language
is so buoyed. Did anyone bring an extension cord?

When the yellow wheat fields are mentioned,
sway your arms back and forth.
Pretend you're in Kansas. I hope
you didn't want a metaphorical moon. Just howl.

Are you familiar with a pork chop in every
Guinness? It's hidden.

And Merwin is just Merwin, Snodgrass is,
you know Snodgrass, and Collins is just
Judy. The singer.

Actually Snow White never had stepmothers.
They were just mothers.

That mountain is actually a Fibonacci valley
of Times New Roman dripping with carbon monoxide.
You know where the dirty gas comes from.

I forgot to mention I've never read here before.
Or anywhere. Let me just say I brought two poems.
This is the shorter one. And I wrote them today.

John Milkereit

The Mudslingers

Stewart and Hondo are the lovers of earth
management tracked by golf carts
sparkling near high clear ground along fence
lines that clip-cut chocolate fields and dirt
roads with spin-splattered thin wheels
on planes of soaking creation driving the
chewed blades of the known down,
but below that surface,
they touch their skin, rub minerals against
their faces to become young again
beneath the undercarriage of vehicles
from chainful tractor pulls and agendas
caked amok. When the rain stops,
they begin to dance in puddles under the double
rainbow with whiskey bottles stuffed in satchels
hidden in their ballooning slickers and
turn, flow across the new light, and leap north
to convey a story of punching stuck goats
north across the Guadalupe River
and into the soft clay of your imagination

John Milkereit

Enter My Honeycombed Vault
after Anila Quayyum Agha's art installation: Intersections

I remember praying
in Pakistan at home, not the mosque,
discomforted as a woman.
The inspiring Alhambra Palace is like my heart,
    a red castle.

In Pakistan at home, not the mosque,
I didn't know laser-cutting wood would lead us
    to confronting boundaries, pure and knife-edged
as my heart, a red castle like the Alhambra Palace,
its rustled leaves, trickled fountains within, even though

confronting our pure and knife-edged boundaries,
    I didn't know would lead to wood laser-cut.
I couldn't resist wiring a 600-watt light bulb.
Even rustled leaves, trickled fountains within,
our shadows intersect these white walls.

I couldn't resist a 600-watt light bulb wired
inside this black box. This sacred space embraces
our shadows that intersect with these white walls.
Now, I wonder if my interior burns or shines.

Inside the embrace, a black box – spaced as sacred
having felt discomforted as a woman,
You entered my honeycombed vault.
    I remember praying.
I shine my interior now, wondrous blur.

John Milkereit

If We Lived at Sarah Oppenheimer's *D-17*

you'd paint the switch plates
under the hammered aluminum roof
even though there is no electricity.

Jutting through glass and brick is what broke apart
as if snow fell and drifted against alleyways.

You'd say we're living under a white, sleek jet wing,
and I wouldn't disagree.

I don't know where you'd hang your dresses.
We've never opened closet doors together.

Windows, who ever needed windows? You'd want rain
droplets falling onto your face even though I'd spiral
into a weathered personality disorder.

I'd want to ski a slope into the entrance
of your heart, but what I learned in
Lake Geneva, Wisconsin failed.

Every elevator pretends I'm an elephant slowly
descending into corners with busted flaps.

Yet this is where we're magnificently crashed.

You'd awaken under a rhombus lifting off mornings.
I'd crust open imbedded parallelograms,
and we'd break boundary layers under the long
neck of this swan.

David M. Orchard

Latitudes and Attitudes

I once heard this quip about North Dakota.
"If you are diagnosed with a terminal illness,
given only one year to live, go to North Dakota.
Go there for longevity. Up there you will be
so bored that one year will feel like ten."
There is a matter of truth in that.

Try this. Go stand on top of Chimborozo, the lofty
Peruvian peak only one and one-half degrees
north of the equator, raise one hand above
your head and spin, spin with the spin of our
globe, one full spin in one full day, in which
time your fingers will travel 24,900 miles, faster
than each and all other fingers on Earth.

Now go eighty-eight and one-half degrees
northward, stand exactly on the North Pole,
stand with arms horizontal and spin, spin
under Polaris, one full spin in one full day,
during which time your fingers will travel a mere
2π times the length of your spine-to-finger reach.

And what about the part of you that is the Pole,
the imaginary vertical line of zero thickness
passing through the center of you. That part of
you is spinning but not moving, going nowhere
at no speed at all. I expect that would be
satisfyingly boring for any dying woman or man.

So, what does that have to do with North Dakota,
half way as it is both down to Peru and up to Pole?
I have been there. I love it there. There, time flies.
It is a matter of velocity, and a matter of philosophy.
It is a matter of latitude, but mostly of attitude.

David M. Orchard

Déjà Vu
for Linda Nolan Hirsch

Nothing within view from the ledge on which I
sat in Wyoming's Big Horn Canyon could have in
any way resembled the hills of home,

certainly not the limestone strata displayed
on the canyon walls, with open caves
superimposed upon the collapsed ruins
of their ancestors of great antiquity,

certainly not the sage, nor the other
aromatic grasses and brush that lent their
scent to the dry air below clear blue sky
and graced my choice of study and career,

and certainly not the wild horses that
I was looking upon when a young man
passed below me, silently striding

diagonally downward, right to left, seemingly
unaware of my presence, certainly unaware
that his passage would cast my mind

across 40 years and 15 degrees of westward longitude
to where she and I sat in mid-fall on Franciscan
chert on a rain-soaked, densely-treed hillside,

where moldering leaves of oak, manzanita, and
madrone lent their scent to soil and air
below passing water-thick Pacific clouds,

to where a young man passed silently
downward right to left below us, seemingly
unaware of our presence, certainly unaware

David M. Orchard

to where a young man passed silently
downward right to left below us, seemingly
unaware of our presence, certainly unaware

of where our minds had been cast by
being together, by the hope for grace
in our coming choices of study and mates.

Michele Vecchitto

Keeper of the Fields

Like his father
and his father before him
This way of life
coursed through his veins

Up before the morning sun
reflected off silos in the fields
Out the door before the kettle
cooled on the word-fired stove

Moving with purpose
he paused briefly to caress
sleepy-eyed barn cats
Meowing their morning greeting

Pitchfork in calloused hands
he swung open a heavy gate
and set to work, his well-worn boots
sinking into the fresh dirt he labored to uncover

Like his father
and his father before him
he worked the fields until the evening sun
lost its battle with the relentless moon

Under a blanket of starry skies
that bathed his land in a soft glow
He rested on his porch, barn cats at his feet
A smile on his lips and satisfaction in his heart

Michele Vecchitto

Reflecting with intent
he paused briefly to give thanks
to a lot in life
that filled him with purpose

Folding dirt-stained hands
that would never quite come clean
He rocked slowly on that creaky porch
surveying his part in the rebirth that is Spring

Like his father
And his father before him
And like his son, folding his own dirt-stained hands
As he rocked beside him.

∞ ∞ ∞

Michele Vecchitto

Dream Receiver

Inspired by prospects of raw freedom, she leaned into every curve
With wind whipping through her loose hair, she never felt more alive
Riding through a winter wonderland, she became a chance believer
She became a dream receiver

The frosty night air caressed her with its magical touch
and each star in the open sky marked possibilities
Leaving miles behind her, she was free
Life was measured in new degrees

Because sometimes it's what's around the next bend
and hidden behind that hairpin turn
that defines a chance believer, a dream receiver
Yesterday is gone

Michele Vecchitto

Bitter Truths

At first touch, minute by minute
worlds are created
built on foundations made from words
slipped from mouths tasting
new experiences

With focused attention lingering
on the unimportant
the solid base is just an illusion
bidding time on shaking ground
as idle hours, lost forever, pass by

Ah, but the power these words hold
Promises laid bare, warm and soft
so blind to the possibility of misplaced trust
Futures are slipping away
slip, slip, slipping away

Somehow those minutes turn
to months turn to years
and worlds intended to be transfigured
become prison cells occupied by
dreams that once offered hope

In that silenced place where all
is seemingly out of touch
and walls close in, suffocating
new worlds are borne, and fresh words are uttered
by a mouth that tastes just a little bitter

Michele Vecchitto

Gratitude

In a time set long ago before clocks ticked away minutes
and days stretched long, anticipating adventures yet created,
gratitude was a sun-soaked sky and the aroma of freshly cut grass
filling the air
Simple was enough and knowing nothing else,
I was thankful

In a time set by clocks sounding alarms for the weary
and days were marked by misadventures, stretching far and wide
gratitude was at best an afterthought in times when survival
outwitted defeat
Chasing complications that were never enough became second
nature
I was remiss

And then I stopped the clock

Sometimes clocks are meant to be broken
Sometimes time is meant to be measured in moments rather than
minutes
Sometimes gratitude is found when time is scarce
Sometimes time is this minute
Sometimes time is now

In a time set by smiles between friends
and hands joined by lovers awaiting the next adventure,
gratitude is a sun-soaked sky and the aroma of freshly cut grass
filling the air
Simple is enough and knowing this is truth
I am thankful

Michele Vecchitto

Our Time

Do you hear time?
Memories disperse like crumbs on water,
hoping to feed the soul's hunger

A need to validate even an inconsequential life

Established with each new breath and defined by the last,
it passes, deliberately partitioning experiences
A rhythmic beat reckons gains and losses

Did it loiter, sweet honey dripping from the hive,
as the comfort of the day murmured reassurance

Did it explode, speeding into the night,
as the search for adventure marked a misspent youth

Did it become suspended, exquisite anticipation
as your trembling lips first whispered *I love you*

Did it consume every breath, punishingly indifferent,
as it ran out for the one that held your heart

I hear time with every tick of the clock
Slivers of yesterday's laughter soothe the sound of long ago tears
Songs in time tell a story only we can write

Entre Deux Souffles

Lorsque le premier souffle de printemps a réchauffé la terre .... elle était ici
Lorsque les premieres neiges d'hiver ont glacé l'air .... elle avait disparu

Lorsque les rayons du soleil ont touché le balcone .... elle était ici
Lorsque le noir est tombé .... elle avait disparu

Lorsque les pêcheurs ont pris la mer .... elle était ici
Lorsque ils ont déchargé leur pêche sur le sable .... elle avait disparu

Lorsque la caravane a apparue par les dunes .... elle était ici
Lorsque il a passé dans la brume .... elle avait disparu

Lorsque une pensée a pris forme dans ma tête ....elle était ici
Lorsqu'elle a quitté ma bouche .... elle avait disparu

Lorsque j'ai allumé une cigarette .... elle était ici
Lorsque je l'ai écrasée .... elle avait disparu

Lorsque je l'ai regardée .... elle était ici
Lorsque je l'ai regardée une deuxième fois .... elle avait disparu

Lorsque j'ai aspiré .... elle était ici
Lorsque j'ai expiré .... elle avait disparu

Une vie, une vie entière,
entre deux souffles.

Between Two Breaths

When the first rays of sunshine stroked the terrace .... she was still there
When the darkness fell over the town .... she had gone

When the fishermen's boats took to the sea .... she was still there
When they emptied their catch on the shore .... she had gone

When the caravan picked its way through the dunes .... she was still there
When it had passed on into the haze .... she had gone

When a thought took shape in my head .... she was still there
When it had formed itself into words .... she had gone

When I lit up a cigarette .... she was still there
When I stubbed it out on the ground .... she had gone

When I looked at her .... she was still there
When I looked at her again .... she had gone

When I breathed in .... she was still there
When I breathed out .... she had gone

A life, a whole life, between two breaths

Camera Obscura
for Andrei Tarkovsky

When he forgot to wind on the film,
when the shutter flicked and stalled and stuttered,
he would say 'it's that camera – it's jammed again'.
He was like that, my father, always someone else's fault.
Until his own life jammed –
or else he forgot to wind it on –
leaving layer upon layer of double exposures.
A pose – just a pose – juxtaposed:
a jumbling of limbs, a tangling of torsos,
his fragmented family, his celluloid boys.
So how is it he's here again,
emulsified into poolside and picnic and balcony vista?
No parallel universe but each to his unique feeling of time.
Because sometimes we're just passing time
and sometimes it's just time passing us.

Someone and Me

I awoke from someone else's dream.
Nothing is ever quite what it may seem.

I inhabited someone else's life.
Took his kid through college, made love to his wife.

Caption on that polaroid reads 'someone and me'.
The image far too faded now to see who that might be.

In everything you worked for, everything you sought.
In your deepest dark desires, in your last unconscious thought.
In the way that you say it and the thing that you say,
My home is in your very bones: I am your DNA.

Mud sinks to the bottom, scum rises to the top.
My ID's in that IV – don't waste a precious drop.

Two electronic heartbeats on that monitor screen.
The one that never was there, the one that might have been.
The splitting of the atom, the splicing of the gene.

And then I awoke from someone else's dream.

Roger West

Whatever Must Come Down, Comes Down Without Going Up

a tocking without a ticking
a screaming without a kicking
a going without a coming
a hawing without a humming
a forgetting without a knowing
an ebbing without a flowing
a power without a prime
a cosine without a sine
an infinity without a zero
an antihero without a hero
an ending without a beginning
a forgiving without a sinning
a knowing without a surmising
a setting without a rising
a metaphysical without a physical
a version without an original

and the clock still tocks but the tick still sticks

Normandy: Haiku

Corrugated clouds
mirror the furrowing fields.
Time folds, time unfolds.

Joyce Gullickson

Feeding Chickens

Each day one more word disappears.
They decompose, first it was *yard birds*,
then *guineas*, *sand* and *dirt*. Horticulture
transposed into hot culture, then just a hot mess.
Word by word, they vanish, even *vanish* is vague.
Feeding chickens, I cannot hear *vultures* circling overhead,
evidence echoes high, as late sun shadows the yard,
the chicken coop is nearly empty.

I recall a vivid dream, a prophecy of sorts. It begins
with feeding chickens, watching you working the wire
mending fences, tending chickens. Wringing the rooster's neck,
the headless torso takes flight, then flops and flaps in the dust.
I feel the body shrinking – *accursed*, and *bloodied*, disappear.
And I am back in catechism, and the teacher is asking
"Where have you been?" I stand accused. Been daydreaming
and my soul is getting smaller. This, my first forgetting –

I've developed an aversion for *eggs*, I peck at breakfast,
my legs are scrawny too. I can no longer grip a pencil.
My letters resemble hen-scratch. I've forgotten the *rules*
of cursive, can't recite the alphabet backwards. The
chicken eludes me as does the body, coming to rest in
the barren fields. I struggle to remember *names, dates,
places, friends*. The greatest commandment, write it down.

Joyce Gullickson

For Clarity's Sake

I do not love you as if you were water or air
or the fragrance of fresh baked bread on the counter.
I love you as the taste of fine wine,
grown fuller with time, its clarity and strength
subtle, smooth, sensual, like the richness
of cedar, set loose by your touch.

Because of you, my rough edges are refined
like a scrap of wood to a whittler's eye.
You see my possibility, the shape of my lines
a bit like Emily's carriage and the fly;
you sense what's inside me, my innermost nature,
your touch as you carve, gentle as the ocean breeze
that freely caresses the trees, and carries the scent
of seaweed, pungent as cedar, fresh and alive.

After Reading Translations of Love

It is good for the body to feel such bliss,
a shared sunset, as seven pelicans glide past.
We watch a lone sand crab confused by the wooden deck,
the flourishes he leaves in the warming sand
as lightning flashes from distant clouds. Across the Gulf
a cargo ship appears… anchored in the vast concurrence
of sun and sand and sky. All those aboard, and us…
silhouettes catching fire.

Hiking the Universe

At cattail marsh, Daddy Long Legs weaves a web
of connection between a berm of broken concrete
and caliche trail. Toxic runoff dribbles into the marsh
staining cattails reddish brown, decay taints the air.
It smells sweet, yet vaguely spoiled. Mud stench seethes
in the summer heat. Our Jack Russell rolls
in onion grass, sniffs appreciatively, then pads
through brackish water, on the trail
of nutria, slick skins gleaming darkly as they sink to safety.

An alligator lazes in the sultry heat, eyes open –
he watches, as if waiting his turn. Today, luck lies with
the duckling paddling into the reeds, out of reach,
and with our dog. His occasional obedience to the master's call
returning him safely to our side. So like a willful child,
learning to survive in this natural wilderness.
A turtle plops into green water and disappears,
I haven't heard a bullfrog's croak in years. We pause to watch
flocks of geese, forgo binoculars for a wider view,
take for granted the beauty of the red-winged blackbird,
the furry black caterpillar, the white egret all co-existing.
As evening approaches the marsh quiets. It's spooky –
Third world dangerous. An owl questions our presence.
Who, who who –
Whose marsh is this? At night the marsh is locked,
behind the chain link fence, the civilized world collapses.

Joyce Gullickson

A Tribute to our Favorite Spot

Our life, lived fully
is a tribute, better left unsaid
for fear, a thief, Nosferatu's shadow (?)
might envy our joy enough
to spitefully sabotage, or plot
to steal our secret…
Imagine your life blood, my soul's marrow
sucked greedily until we, You and I
no longer survive. Imagine, Imagine
our favorite spot on the stair,
Imagine our physical selves no longer there.
As we join the undead, become smoke and ash
all that's left of our flesh and bone.
Now imagine our spirits holding hands
on the stairway from heaven
halfway up, halfway down
holding hands, holding hands
where our journey began.

April 21, 2016
for Prince

that day a chasm rips through
      me like your electric riffs

that carve me open every time, haunting
      more thoroughly

than any ghost. you can hardly blame
      my heart for its fatal lurch

into those eyes of yours
      that smoke me out

all my devil, all my angel
      baptize broken me whole again

with truths my bones moan. scientists say
      the stars we wish upon

take so long to appear clear to us
      that they've died out long ago.

what we see is not the star, but an image
      of the star as it was

while it was burning itself alive. how strange
      to live under a false sky. I think you

were never here. I think you never left.
      chasm, space between, fire, oxygen

Aimee Mackovic

Dare
for Prince

Two months to the day of your passing
is the summer solstice set against
the backdrop of a full moon called strawberry
the last time that happened was 1967
summer of love a time when
the tilt of the earth's axis is most inclined
towards the sun, towards the heat, towards molten
change when there are less shadows to hide
from the dawdling daylight and the light
for me it is a Tuesday with no classes to teach
so I grade papers in a coffee shop for hours
reading students' stories about abuse and neglect
and how can I possibly sieve such words into a grade
so I just drink coffee while my pen apologizes
later I go to yoga melt into my mat ask it to take over
while I rest my brain everything is askew
nowadays so helter skelter is the world
that merely breathing is a dull blade to the soul
just existing is hot lava in the marrow
the poet Jamaal May writes *dare doesn't mean*
the same thing when you dare yourself
does it? Of course he is right as the sun succumbs
to moon as dark takes over light I drive you sing
about sex and love and life I dare my blood outright
to mean something to squeeze the stardust hiding
out of every single oceanic breath

Aimee Mackovic

Tattoos and Scars

Not even forty-eight hours after
news broke of how your energy
decided to swap out its human canvas
slip through the aperture I'm sitting
in a tattoo shop in a strip mall in Texas
my third tattoo so the mellifluous hum
of the machine soothes my ears
my chatterbox mind as we all pretend
this is actually permanent that the ink
will last that it even matters it won't
some studies say that people with tattoos
are happier than those without theory being
that tattoos help heal emotional scars
that the voracious needles poke the pain
till it pops subcutaneously bursting
into art on flesh I thumb your love symbol
now upon my wrist think how wonderful
to be able to wear a wound so perfectly

Aimee Mackovic

Purple Vesper
I'll celebrate the day I die: Prince

Paisley Park. 10:07am.

death: architect
of freedom. weeps kiss the world
spectacularly ecstatic.

soul blend, runaway, jazz living,
You
romance the opening. transformation.

heavy darling, lead the moon
and battle beautiful.

You: triumphal masterpiece.

Aimee Mackovic

Self Portrait as Gigi, Favorite Childhood Doll

Time can flirt with me all she wants,
but she'll never get her way, her ghost touch
swirling around me, but never lethal.
Little I've changed in thirty years watching you
try on a thousand masks, catapult your heart
from city to city, burn yourself to ashes
over and over again, swallow the thorns
of lover's exits, and come begging for more.
If anything in your life
has been constant, it's been me and my red velvet dress
splattered with silver sequins
that you coveted, the forever of my eyes
tuned always to the now, the jagged tear
in my left hand where you chewed a hole,
hungry for things you could not then name.
It is an honor to savor this coat of dust,
maroon myself on your shelf, flex my feet
to the dying stars, and be the silent anchor
stringing all your *yous* together, the sponge
of thoughts unspoken, deft root
of countless lifetimes notched
haphazard upon slick, tempestuous bones.

Aimee Mackovic

Requiem for a Kiss

Caught somewhere between our prickled flesh
and the blistering point of no return

there was lip on lip, there was headspace
gone cloudy and amok, there was a flash of words

that smacked and snarled, there was the unhidden gist
of it all summed up in the electric jungle

of your deep mahogany eyes that dared to cast me
away once again, make of my wits and soul

a reckless phantom. My bones have never been
magnetized to such a danger. Though under shadow

of a lush moon fraught in dazzling alabaster, we let go,
there will never be a breath I take that does not plummet

the depth you loiter in me, never be a kiss
that is not laced with memory, never be a love

that did not spring from this self you helped morph
into this living vesper, choking with sparkle and hot scars.

Jim Parker

Preincarnated

If I could be preincarnated
I would stand atop a mountain
trumpet in hand; back arched, mute in place
loftin' sweet sounds across the sky for Miles and Miles
Workin', Relaxin', Cookin', & Steamin'

I would stand at the front of the river boat,
barefoot, bare-chested, bold and brassy
booming "Mark Twain"
as I beat my young boy pecs

I would lie in the grass
and play with Walt's beard
and to our dirty hearts' delights
we would sound off our barbaric yawps-yawp, yawp, yawp

I would croon with Ella
and she would teach me how to scat
scoobity doobity boo bop bop bop a rebop

I would lyricize with Langston
working together to defy the deferral of any dreams

I would jump train with Sandburg
noticing passing landscape set to music on his guitar

I would drink whiskey, droppin' words with Papa
in the most northern parts of the upper peninsula

and I would find both of you
and I would assure you that everything was going to be all right
and that I would grow up to be just fine

Jim Parker

The Gift of Pottery

On the outside, baby blue bleeds into beige
On the inside, oft I will leave this gifted bowl empty
Its smooth deep interior reminds me of possibility

Now full,
The painting might be titled "Still Life Bowl of Assorted Chocolates"
Always a reminder though

You, who gave such a gift,
Crafted by your own hands
also created a beautiful Thanksgiving day
of patchwork family, football, bierocks, and Scrabble

Now just a memory
Our ways parted
Our lives push us forward
But the bowl serves as a reminder
People can create such Beauty in this world
and in emptiness there is infinite Possibility

Molcajete

As a boy,
the word molcajete was not in my vocabulary
nor really were the words tradition, nor heirloom, nor identity
seeking tradition, seeking consistency
mi esposa of ten years gifted me ancient cultural cookware
and now, I rinse and grind, rinse and grind, rinse and grind,

Jim Parker

how to compete with a century old family heirloom though,
to smooth the surfaces of rock on rock in so short a time

As a boy,
five moves in five years
change was familiar, and familiar was foreign
seeking identity, seeking meaning
Now I attempt to smooth the surface
I grind and rinse, grind and rinse, grind and rinse
until the pain of callous opens bleeding on my palm
My self-created stigmata

As a teen,
I desired roots that could not be torn up and transplanted,
so I created my own traditions
I created my own patchwork quilt,
the one my grandmother never passed down to me
But identity comes at a price-
solid memories started when I ran far enough away to begin forgetting
Grind and rinse, grind and rinse, grind and rinse

As a man,
I remember what I forgot
Grind and rinse
Callouses heal
Grind and rinse
surfaces smooth
Grind and rinse
water runs clear,
it is time to season;
time to create new memories,
It is time

Jim Parker

Awakened Man

Expansive night sky canvas is splayed with colors and patterns
as the multitude stands, eyes upward in awe
The air is alive with energy and anticipation
What comes next?

Brimming with this same energy and anticipation
the Awakened Man, filled with possibility
You edge up to the precipice of today and shout
What comes next?

Demons, depravity, and depression are jettisoned into night sky
exploding in rageful reds and bottom-of-the-barrel blues, dissipating into the darkness
your immortal soul now free to choose its own colors and patterns
What comes next?

There is past, and that's where it lives
There is future, and that's where it lives
There is infinite possibility, and that is where you live

Confident in this infinite possibility, you can also sit
Your presentation of presence becomes our present of presence
as we too are allowed to sit with you and be
This is now

And for now, the canvas of the night sky is splayed with colors and patterns
and those of us who know you and who love you
Will sit in wonder and awe, and we will ponder
What comes next?

Vapor

To have you neither completely here
Nor fully there
Is the hardest step
In this process of leaving
For I cannot communicate
With you in my former lazy way,
Half-attending to your words.
I must adapt
To your new style
Without sound
Without eyes.

Easel

I paint a new picture of death
Because death is an art
Not a science.

It is a portrait
Of a new acquaintance
You are also painting for me.
It is two-dimensional,
For you and I do not yet know him well.

Still, he is
Not a grotesque gargoyle
Hung on a museum wall,
But a member
Of the family
So to speak
In a bedroom
Eager to help.

Surprising, Isn't It?

You
Are here
In spite of circumstances
Hindrances
In spite of *yourself*
You
Are here
A strong cord has tethered you
Something of umbilical strength
Defying age
Interest
Intention
Drawing you
Gathering you in
Picking you up
Causing you
Of all people
To have hope again
Just a shred
A scrap
But enough
To stitch around
To fashion a new garment
Serviceable
Malleable
Warm
Go ahead
Try it on for size.

Pre-Retirement Mail

If storks deliver
Bundles of joy and work and worry,
Then today
The albatross arrived
With forms
To help us ruminate
Fodder for our futures
As we are led out to pasture.

Claire Vogel Camargo

Riverstone Words

Riverstone words flow
in tumbling disarray
off the tongue, propelled
by the swirling current.
        They pitch and roll, turning
        with glisten and glow, in a
        rhythm and angle only they
        can know or find.

Riverstone words in many
colors, textures, and forms:
smooth, rough, sharp, round;
feeling just so on the mind.
        Some hurt, some no; some pink,
        tan, or black; some pebbles, cairns,
        or paperweights; some fitting in
        the hand, heart, or soul.

Riverstone words meandering
through the waters of one's mind;
free-flowing, gently bumping,
or crashing over turbulent rapids.
        Spread like caviar over riverbeds
                        and garnish on
riverbanks, they
        declare existence and reveal
        the geology of our lives.

Claire Vogel Camargo

Adrift

My History of Western Thought teacher in high school
spoke of other dimensions of place and time. His eyes
sparkled gray-blue, hands lifted – palms turned skyward,
as he paced in front of the class.

His body seemed to quiver as he articulated alien ideas
such as, "These desks are not here. You are not here.
You just think you are."

*How does this concept relate to history or the West?
Can it be true? How does he know? Is he talking about
philosophy or science?*

uncomfortable
floating in space, I forgot him –
until now

wonder
where he was from –
besides Earth

Jonathan Harrington

Listening to Stones

I listen to the trees
murmuring and mumbling
but I cannot quite make out
what they are trying to tell me.

Birds are more intelligible.
It's almost as though we speak the same language.
Their territorial shrieking at dawn
is easily understood
and their longing and desire
at dusk
their pitiful cooing to be loved.

But stones are almost mute.
I rarely hear them say anything.
They just sit there, tolerant
of almost everything: rain, heat, cold
being hurled at squirrels by brats,
even being stepped on.

That is the way I want to become:
mute and dumb
and to chase from my mind
all this thinking, thinking, thinking
that really does nothing
but jumble up my head
and obstruct my view of the world.

Now I know where that expression must come from
…you know…
I guess I am a kind of hippie.

I just want to be stoned.

Jonathan Harrington

Wilderness

Deeper and deeper
you go into the wilderness
to live a life apart.
You make a dwelling of rock
a table, a log for a chair.
A spoon, a cup, a metal bowl,
the only remnants
from that far-off life,
abandoned long ago.
As the years turn moon by moon
you find the wilderness much deeper,
much busier than you had imagined.
Each day you struggle to invent
a reason to breath
to eat, to drink.
Each day, each year
the wilderness grows deeper.
You begin to see a god
in the face of every tree, rock, and star.
You go deeper and deeper
until finally you enter
that most frightening
and solitary jungle of all –
that wilderness
within us.

Turning Sixty

I will almost certainly never
play line-backer for the Dallas Cowboys.
I may never go back to Tunisia
to explore the ruins of Carthage.
I see enough ruin
each morning in the mirror.
I will not be climbing Mt. Everest.
I am reasonably certain
I will never sleep with Jennifer Lopez
– but what the hell – it's *her* loss.
I could still parachute
out of a light plane over Patagonia
or go hang gliding over the Copper Canyon
or bungee jumping in Botswana
but I don't want to do any of that anyway.
The only extreme sport that interests me is sex
every once in a while until that is gone, too.
I can't chat with Jorge Luis Borges
about epistemology or the etymology
of the Bulgarian word for carrot
in a café in Buenos Aires while sipping mate
because Borges has already gone on.
I will never smoke opium
with Lithuanian expatriates in Kathmandu –
not that I couldn't
but at 60 you must decide
what it is you *really* want to do
with the time god has loaned you
until the balloon payment is due.
I will never be the president of the United States of America
though I still have a shot
at president of the local poetry society.

I may yet write a great poem
although I know it's not this one.
I may still live to see humans
set up housekeeping on Mars
but I will not be inhabiting
any space-colonies, thank you.

Questions About Glass

What exactly is glass?
And don't tell me the science of it,
I'm not talking about that.
How is it that something you can see straight through
that is almost invisible,
can knock you out
if you run into it?
The swallow that tried to fly through
my window yesterday at dusk
and broke its neck –
Is that supposed to be a metaphor for something?
You can't blame the swallow.
It was only trying to pass from one side
of an invisible shield to another
and gave its life trying.
Think about when glass shatters
into a thousand tiny blades
that can wound you.
Was it invented for that purpose?
Or is it just a flaw in its composition?
Smooth as glass?
Yeah, right.
Shatter it and you can slice your wrists.

Jonathan Harrington

It's an enigma, this stuff, glass.
And don't get me started on mirrors.
Then things get very complicated.
So much of the world we see
is framed by glass.
It has the power to draw attention to things
such as that bougainvillea
framed by my kitchen window
as if the glass is confining it, defining it, for me.
The last time I left you at the airport
I watched you from my side of the glass door
as you disappeared on your side.
And though I could not have articulated it at the time
I might have asked, like a child:
When you are on your side of the glass
and I'm inside,
like a convict on visiting day,
I can see you,
I can even hear you,
but why can't I touch you?

Jonathan Harrington

The Fallen

That tree just beyond my bedroom window,
barely noticed here in the wilderness surrounded by trees.
It clung to an escarpment
its roots hugging a rock so tightly
it had become a part
of that rock – needed it, embraced it, could not live without it.
Then, again without my noticing,
it fell
as I went about my busy, solitary life
on some other part of the property.
Only then, days later
did I discover it laid out, fallen
taking with it
a piece of that rock
which it had held onto for life.
Only then did I notice its enormous beauty
as it lay prone
on its back, face up.
Does a tree have a face?
I examined with care
its muscular branches
its fragile leaves,
its graceful, dead body.
Why, why? I asked myself…
Why does it take death
for us to finally see
and begin to love
a tree, a rock, a face?

Still Life

There is no one waiting
back home.
Nor is there really a "back"
nor in any sense a home.
Simply this:
a table, a chair,
a tin cup, a tin bowl, and a spoon,
carefully arranged,
waiting mutely
for no one
in the dying light.
of almost everything: rain, heat, cold
being hurled at squirrels by brats,
even being stepped on.

Gilbert Juergens III

What It's All About

It is all about
rebirth, the sudden
sprouting of hidden undergrowth.

It is all about
umbilical scars and scars
on the face of the man in the moon,

and the wanting, the wanting
more than a life beyond stars
or a bite of time, a rib, a future.

If only   If only   If only

It is all about
dust and what becomes of it
when pushed by west winds,

when muddied,
when squeezed in the hands
beyond hands.

First you, then me, then us
together and wanting beyond wanting,
breathing new life beyond living.

Life Beginning

When earth was the sole language,
dreaming in its watery bed
and watching stars, listening
to the Morse code of rain
tell it about the universe,
there was no cadence
at its core

Not until a single cell wrapped
its sheath around a raindrop
and drew blood from salt
was there another voice,
a conversation about
life beginning and
speculation

That there were other dreams,
dreams without boundaries
that could not be heard
on earth or in its seas,
dreams waiting
for dreamers

Gilbert Juergens III

Revenir

Remains
laid bone-to-bone
beneath chiseled words
on cracked stone

splinter when spirits
return and arrange them
into sentences that protest
the dark forest,

the poverty of mortality
in a universe that seems
to go on and on in a spiral
of half-starts and full-halts.

They are brittle,
these remains, confined
to afterwards and underfoot
in a world designed

for the future
of nimble creatures
whose time is measured
by births and deaths;

who must wonder
what revenants would
gain by the impermanence
of life above ground
and whether an assured hereafter
is without a lingering doubt
life's final chapter.

When Death Prevails

we will have
no use for
the pickled
fruit of life

our faces
will simply
melt into
the cracks
of the universe

we who
clutch
the earth with
talon claws

have
sorrow settle
on our shoulders
like autumn mist
onto yellowed leaves

we will no longer
be tormented
except by eternal mysteries

Gilbert Juergens III

Night Skies

what if moon
were sun's disguise
when it no longer
lights the skies
when day is ending soon?

what if stars
and the planet Mars
were balloons launched
in years gone by
to calm the fears
of primal man?

and all around us
nature was nothing
but a ball of fur
rolled into one large sphere
just because   because

there is no power
no other what-ever
that rules us here
in this place held dear
by us and all our selves
stretched back to
when and after then?

Patricia Young Smith

Unpacking for the Trip

Let's get this straight
I don't want to hang around
And pick white lint from
Life's ruddy velvet when I am,
As they call it, gone

I travel light
Empty my pockets –
Little mirror, thirty-dollar Times
A grasshopper's elegant leg.
Opinions like carved ivory buttons
Tumble down. With a drift of song
Pockets go, too.
Jettison the body
Whee!
All candy and no wrapper.

On the darkened path
Nothing to wear but my karma.

James B. Nicola

Have You Ever Woken

Have you ever woken up, after a loss,
and gone outside, and found there such a mist
of morning – of mourning – that you thought you
were somewhere else, that the loss wasn't lost,

and then you heard a voice from far away
whisper your name, then, vocative, pierce through
the mist and guide you back to what you knew
once, where you were, how things had been? You toss

left, toss right, and wake up again, only
to find there is no mist, no voice, no day,
there is no Is, because there is no We
anymore? You have? I have too, and say

I'm your friend, even if we've never met,
here to help you forget, and not forget.

The Wrong Place

The wrong place at the wrong time –
    don't two wrongs make a right?
At least, don't double negatives
    like *not not* or *not night*

imply a glimmer in the gloom,
    a slack in Fate's flung rope
that her hungry noose might be slipped from
    by a hummingbird of hope?

Now, *the wrong place at the* right *time,*
    and *the right one at the wrong,*
are eggs that hatch a darker bird
    who'll sing a tragic song –

a raven caught in a beaver trap,
    or starling, crow, or chough
that craves and strays like the man who wants
    and cannot have enough.

But *wrong-wrong* is a circumstance
    of plot complexity
that upside-downs the grimaced mask –
    a cause for comedy.

James B. Nicola

Friends Strangers Multitudes

I ran into someone I knew from years ago
in Trafalgar Square once; another, at the Taj Mahal,
where there were myriads, and thought, how many did I know
that I never ran into, but were there? And should I inspect all

of them? Another time I met a stranger on a train,
and we're friends still – which we'd not be, had I sat one seat away.
Another time, I ducked indoors downtown, when it started to rain,
and there stood the person I'd marry – we're married to this day –

who, when we're on vacation in New York, say at Times Square,
or other crowded tourist sites in Paris or in Rome,
and I think about saying hello to everybody there,
reminds me it's not wise, if we plan on getting home.

James B. Nicola

Traces

It's neither déjà vu nor quite, a dream.
Their number is the same, only their faces,
the few that I can see, aren't what they seem,
not human beings, really, but the traces

of sandlots where my home-run saved the day,
now tamed in asphalt for a mini-mall;
of side yards where we used to play croquet,
the yard too narrow now, the grass too tall

for play. A plastic sign covers the old
bank's name, deep-chiseled in the crumbly lime.
Inside, teenagers, part-timers, refold
bright shirts with care, to try on one more time.

The traffic does not slow around the square
but, breathing only air-conditioned air,
goes windows up, as in an armored car,
dark-spectacled. I can't see who they are

and close my eyes. In a flash, everyone
is back, and tramps the lawn, and scales the stone
for Joe to chase us off, always in fun,
and benches fill with souls as they did when
I lived here. When I open them again,
I'm back, adult, alive, alert, alone.

Neil Meili

Quantum Lunch

There is nothing stable in this table

And yet
the ever so quickly spinning
nothingness
that is me
is happy this particle-wave
filled morning
to rest on it with non-existent elbows
and gaze and gaze
at the improbable you

Rule Britannica

Mostly musty now
Google-buried deep
in library stacks and garage
sale *Take it for a Dollar* boxes

Generations
denied the pleasure
of sitting with a volume
rich and heavy to the hand

and knowing you could know
everything there was to know
about whatever started with an M
to whatever started somewhere with an O

Neil Meili

Dante's 9th Inning Stretch

In life there are errors
errors and regrets
and then there is baseball

The ball off the end of the glove
the errant throw, any errant throw

The running into the other fielder
and the ball dropping between

The not being willing
to run into the other fielder
and the ball dropping between

The not tagging up at third

The easy dribbler down the first base line
and knees that won't let you bend to pick

The ball that was called a strike
the strike that was called a ball

For Catholics there's Purgatory
with constant replay of regret

For baseball fans
there's late October to forever

Neil Meili

Ode to NASA

The astronauts heard the music
on the far side of the moon

Think of that tonight
when you dance in her light

Dr. Charles A. Stone

Simplicity

THE magic that plays music
for the dance that holds us in place
after we have used up our skin
in a lifetime of holding hands,
skinning shins and dancing
is rarely more complex
than the blurred images
of parallel universes
spinning away from
the central core
of life.
STARS
falling away
and suns melting
moons that wander
too close to sail through
cryptic skies of the Milky Way
are no more mysterious than gravity
is to the apple that slips free of its tree
before leaves change color in the fall,
or the steady swing of a metronome
as it measures our stay on earth.

Dr. Charles A. Stone

Fout-Ta-Ta-Rou

the mitral valve collapsing
among heartbeats
fout-ta-ta-rou
snow falling
on thin skin of frozen ponds
fout-ta-ta-rou
an axe
severing the grasp of trees
to earth
fout-ta-ta-rou
swings
without children
plagued by relentless wind
fout-ta-ta-rou
a glutinous sauce
bubbling
fout-ta-ta-rou
footsteps
retreating in dawn's
early light
fout-ta-ta-rou
a keyboard
attacked by 2 fingers
fout-ta-ta-rou
echoes of galaxies
colliding
yours -and- mine
fout-ta-ta-rou

Dr. Charles A. Stone

Because the Bible Tells Me So

```
we are not floating through          space
   on a light bulb
                                     waiting for someone to
paint
                                        hands on the face
                                     of our mortal clocks
no…                                  we are tap  tap  tapping
                                     on the thin shell beneath
                                          our feet
parting the topsoil                  ,curious as Moses
to see what the sea bed is about…
                                     looking for hieroglyphics…
hoping for a message between the lines
      of rain\\bows                  tap tap      tapping
      listening for echoes…

         telling stories             about
             candied apples in trees
                                          (serpents playing
tambourines
                                             (mice dancing
and all the while                    taptaptapping
                                     on earth's crust…

waiting                              ,hoping   ,telling stories
      tap
            tap      tapping)
```

Throughout the Long Night

  it cannot be seen
by you
        it cannot be seen
    that consumes
turns to ash

                        or others…
            the fire
            me
            our love
            for one another…

                  what others   believe
of spirits merging   lost in dust
            cannot be seen
            or tasted
  on the tips of tongues on which we
                  float…

w e are
                moon and sun   fire
            and water   we cannot be
heard
  without doubt raging in ears
                unaccustomed to
truth…
            truth we carry in buckets
from world to world from earth to sky…
              riding on the breath of
            dreams
and lost in fingerprints of time
            like melting snowflakes
                  like melting snowflakes

Haunting

heartbeats you hear
when I am asleep
are spirits haunting
my dreams

when I am asleep
memories percolate beneath the surface
where they

are spirits haunting
the passages from this life to the next
and in these passages

my dreams
allow me to move freely from
alpha to omega

Dr. Charles A. Stone

In Hospice

Their eyes explore the darkness
        their ears quake in the silence
And their fingers   their fingers
        brush lightly against the bark of their skin
All this as they stare at the open door
        beyond which a great twilight swirls
And parallel universes collide
        parallel universes that clutch
The spirits of those lost in time
        lost in a tide of emotion
Between day and night
        searching for secret passageways
Through eternity while holding tight
        corporeal crutches that tether them
To a world whose consequence
        no longer matters   no longer matters

Who We Are

I know now the dark is not infinite,
stars might fall and the moon
is a paper-thin perversion of the sun...

The wind, a cruel breath from the earth's
lungs, carries not only daydreams of poets,
but pages of metaphors describing the skies...

The shapeless skies outlined above by clouds
and below by trees whose branches are inscrutable
as the dark reverberations of night creatures...

Beachcombers, those who drag gunny sacks
of shells across tortured shoals, know too well
the shifting fate of skies and sand...

Know too well the destiny of civilizations
at the edge of seas, deciphering
the place of man in the universe...

While poets continue to describe loneliness
in the slate grey eyes of sparrows and death
in the mournful call of coyotes...

While astronomers search the edge of dark
for clues about the birth and death of stars and
speculate about who we are...

Dr. Charles A. Stone

Songs of Newborns

I am the future reaching
                        for strength…
                        for knowledge

My dreams are open
                        to the skies above…
                        I am innocent
                        as the moon's dark side
                        and unknown to man

My mother's kisses
                        disguise the truth…
                        she cries for my soul
                        counts her tears
                        and prays   for times past

She listens for the echo
                        of truth
                        in things I learn to say…
                        they will taunt her
                        throughout her life…

My grasp is a reflex
                        the sudden realization
                        that her time has passed…
                        she is invincible
                        no more…

Dr. Charles A. Stone

Beyond the Door

Beyond the door is an orchard

of silent trees

backlit by a radiance that few

remember seeing

in the life that preceded this one

but which is

the gauze upon which old women

rest their heads

after their men, their husbands

and their sons,

have been bled from the earth

set adrift on the sea

The dark limbs of the trees

are motionless,

their leaves resting on

the barren earth

of dioramas visible from the door

where they mingle

in shadows with forgotten dreams

and cast-off hopes

of those who haunt the orchard

in the endless night

and whose presence is known

by the smell of incense

Glynn Monroe Irby

Phosphor Nights

There are dreams
when full streams flow
into the lake edge,
when night owls
fly silently searching,
when the long moon ripples
from the flesh-ends
of my fingertips,
and albino bison clash
their dark horns together

The Swan Goose

Crossing the unfolding tundra
on my ancestral Baltic train
in powerful motion, I stand alone,
bracing myself for strength
against the cold constant flow
of arctic air that forces itself
through the opened window row
and curls past me incessantly
icing the minor veins within my fingertips
and crystallizing the moisture on my lips.
As the light just barely breaks
into the chilling mist, and still
the brighter morning stars exist
in the darker indigo
of the far northwestern sky,
the golden double set of rails

Glynn Monroe Irby

curve around a narrow finger lake.
Suddenly on the opposite side
was the silver glow
of a single swan
sliding along the shore
through an early haze
before a stand of conifer trees.
My spirit then traveled
to another time and place
within my memory, arousing
quick illusive images of frozen ponds
and pale blue walls of ice
at the highland passages
and stalking with sure deliberation
at the seductive moors
to embrace the beautifully illusional
white-ivory swan goose
under the translucent colors
of the multi-ribboned portal
into my subconsciousness
and so elegant in the shallow fog
over the wintry surface
of the streams in my imagination.
Abruptly my attention was torn away
by angled ferrous trestle beams
snapping past my window frame
as the railcar clanked across
an aging wood-iron bridge
between the world of hers
and the world of mine.
I felt different then.
Strangely more enriched.
I'd been a part
of a sacred scene
-- as in life –
although only momentarily,

Glynn Monroe Irby

impatient, beyond control,
but none-the-less a sacred scene.
And I felt different then.
Some many years removed,
on my journey home
in another continent,
I saw the swan again
where she had chosen to be
during a cold-blue norther
out of place past midnight
on a pond of chemical waste
beside petroleum distillation towers
standing eerily in illumination
from sodium vapor lamps
and in the sultry amber steam
over the warm effluence –
I saw her
swimming alone,
and she even then
was beautiful.

Glynn Monroe Irby

Jump-Fly Journeys

It's disconcerting, some say,
to see large men jump up
and drift gently through space
not more than ten feet in the air
in speeds exceeding only slightly
the normal hiking rate,
as often I do in the late night
or sometimes just at dawn.
It's mostly a matter of faith
that I take in air and fly at all.
But every minute or so,
as always it goes,
to fly still farther on my course,
it's necessary to renew my leap.
I cross this way
the fences, and gullies,
the fields, and thoroughfares,
and if judging just right
I skirt above
the wider edges of lakes.
On occasion, though,
I jump-fly higher than limbs.
And in rocky hills
even higher than cathedral rings.
Although I suspect,
were I to fly there long,
I'd certainly slip out
of my perspective and sight.
While most often I come lightly
to the ground, sometimes I come down
pitching forward too far
tumbling my arms, and legs, and eyelids apart
to see again the frozen first sleet
of still another season.

Imagi 06

As a winding spring animates
the separate hands of motion —
so the measured heart
carries the quarried spirits
into yesterday.
As immaculate sand trickles
past a narrow swirl of glass —
the alabaster hours of this day
slip through the hands
of timelessness.

Lynn Wheeler-Brandstetter

Timeless Travel

I wonder if the universe gasps
When I close my eyes
And my soul begins timeless travel

Travel whose destiny is different
For each season, wisdom that changes
With each dimension I enter

My soul floats above the abyss
Savoring a taste of eternity
Searching the lace of infinity

For footprints I leave behind
When my eyes open to new days
And I turn outward to elusive time

Georg Reilly

Celestial Plan

Until lightning purges
the night sky of stars
or the ominous rumble
behind clouds portends
something more than rain,

I will marvel at the magic
synapses between
the universes we inhabit,
as though our being here
is part of a celestial plan.

In my watchful waiting
for the next intersection
of our separate spheres,
I will roll dice and count
bones which tell of promises

That there is no randomness
in our spinning through time,
waiting for piano keys and
guitar
strings to equalize the pressure
between your music and my
song.

Georg Reilly

Mist of Time

loving you is not
enough to pull you
from empty dreams
into my life

nor is wanting you
sufficient to bring
us together across
invisible barriers

that keep separate
the worlds in which
we flounder through
the mist of time

perhaps this is why
i search the eyes
of strangers during
chance encounters

perhaps this is why
i know things
about others before
i really know

what experiences
we have shared, before
i whisper to lovers
when we part:

moving through time
with you at my side
is not the same as
being with you

Georg Reilly

More Than Dreams

the exotic west wind pursues
dandelion parachutes

lazy shadows chase willowy trees
into the forest as the sun sets

falcons hurry after shiftless clouds
suspended above a bedeviled earth

squirrels leap from branch to branch
as autumn wood snaps to attention

brightly colored trout lazily scour
currents clear as gypsy crystal

but none of these familiar exploits
is conducted with the urgency

of my search of the universe
for affirmation that you are there

and are here from time to time
under *my* sky   under *your* sky

Generation XO

humanity
decays slowly

--

our faults will have
revenge

--

the future will be lost
in our footprints

--

nothing will survive
our greed

--

no seed will survive
the pursuit of idols
and trinkets

--

we will be victims
of our lies
will lose everything

--

we will be blind mice
running
out of time

Georg Reilly

Trapped in Time

We are trapped in time

That changes too quickly
For our minds to adjust

In a place that changes
Too slowly for our eyes

In a universe reaching
Too far for travel

But is too close to truth
For us to understand

Why we met once
And may never meet again

The Buoyancy of Light

A blistered moon falls around a blasted landscape
Where lonely, thin winds try to move grains of sand around
Where once a shallow ocean rippled brightly,
And nurtured strange creatures in the shallows and deeps.

But for a million years or more the rocks had forgotten
What humidity felt like, and knew only dust
And thin winds,
And silence.
But still the moon rolled past, night after night,
Playing its pale beams over the sands, looking,
Sending seductive waves of gravity,
Pulling at abandoned places,
Reaching out to nothingness
With the buoyancy of light.

The Tunes of Life

All those years ago
And I still remember the first time,
In the moonlight,
When you stood before me
Shy, uncertain, serene,
While I tried to start breathing,
Soaking in the sight of you
With your gown fallen, body free.
All these years, as you leaned in
Asking me to find the music,
To clumsily compose songs of our life,
Teaching me how it should go,
With you as the instrument upon which
Our song would be played.

Birds Make Holes in Heaven

Birds make holes in Heaven
Through which our souls may fly.
This morning mine fluttered and flapped,
Struggled to gain altitude against
The anchors of memory and attitude.
I think it's time to take the dog
Out to the forest again, watch her lose herself
In the Mountain Laurel and streams,
To find happiness in her true self.
I'll walk behind her to where
I'm going, and stand still, like the Blue Heron,
Who misses nothing in the stream, waiting for
Uplifting breezes.

North of Tombstone, 3 AM

Shadows and silhouettes backed by a waning moon
Slide past like California's promises,
Distant and confusing.
Off to the south, somewhere over the sand and arroyos and cacti
Is Old Mexico. A few miles, no more.

A small town slips into view,
Safeway. Ace Hardware.
Benson Fuel glares at a Shell station on the other corner.
Ten-thousand tons glide to a stop so softly it would not wake a baby with colic.
An old woman with a bonnet lifts her travel bag over the curb,

Joining our travels. Where can she be going, alone? El Paso?
Chemo, hoping it works this time?
Or just to visit her daughter?
Her husband watches as she gets on board,
His hands shoved in jeans pockets, looking dried out like the land...
Then turns back to the pickup for the long
Drive home in the dark, first stopping for coffee, for something
warm to hold.

Rolling again, now, eastward toward a slice of New Mexico, then
El Paso and Texas.
The car rocks softly, the miles drift by, the engine far ahead
The horn blast at crossings is barely heard.
I wonder about the kind of man who would come here
In the early times, on horseback, or on foot
Across this lonely place that only wanted to suck the water from
him.
Was it silver? Land? Water?
Or simply that those men had just run
All other choice in life away,
And this dry place, full of ghosts and questions,
Was the last that would take them,
And cared for nothing
But the water in them.

All Is Temporary

I'm nearly old, she said… to no one,
Before the mirror,
Tracing a line down her cheek
With a fingertip,
Lost in memory.
She sighs.
A chill; her soul shivers.
This is the face that boys
Longed to kiss, she remembers,
Remembering the power of it.

Yet now the boys are men, although not as many.
The face that felt the chubby caress of
Her children's hands,
The face she could depend upon.
A breeze ruffles the curtains,
Touches the flower beside the mirror.
Her eye caresses the exquisite
Design of it, built for
A moment
Of perfect purpose.
"You are nearly old, too," she says, tracing the edge of the
Petal with her finger.
She smiles, newly aware…
All things must pass.
All things are temporary.

Breathe Briefly

We breathe so briefly of Life,
Of spring days and summer rains,
And winters' nights – all too quickly gone.

Our years fly away like ash
From a dying campfire,
Lost in the darkness
Fluttering up to the stars.

Yet in our days
We feel and think and wonder,
Love, and grieve loves lost,
Enfold our children in our arms
Until they fly.

The flames and embers of the fire,
Alive, dancing, shifting, speaking to primal things,
Fill my mind with
Thoughts of eternity.

I lean in, looking for signs
And visions
And warmth.

Nuart (Nvard Chalikyan)

The Mystery of the Universe

And the whole universe,
With its timeless mysteries,
Its shining stars and lonely black holes,
With billions of particles
Scattered across light-years
in a fusion of life and death,
of illusive beginnings and ends,
of dark and light,
light and dark,
cold and warm,
heat and maze,
thrill and blaze
and music
of human hearts…
energy,
dreams,
passions of life…
the almighty desire of existence…
and the possibility of everything, always, ever…

All of it shrank,
became one
and cuddled itself
into a small, tiny circle
all in one,
all – here

in the eyes
of a newborn child!

Nuart (Nvard Chalikyan)

Be There
(Between My Sun and My Clouds)

Be the home of my soul on earth
Where my soul can rest its head,
Be in this airless space between my sun and my clouds,
So that I lose my fear of death.

Be high within me,
Be tall within me,
So that I never have to stoop
Or be less than what I am,
So that I grow tall towards you,
So that I glow bright towards you…

Live there – amid the unspoiled and unnoticed,
So that I know I have untrodden snow-white places inside me
To which I can come… secretly.
Date me there
In that holy place, in the only place that's real,
So that my spirit flies to you
With closed eyes,
With wings fully open,
With a mountain taste in its mouth,
With its nightingale song
Sung for you alone, away from the crowd...

Please be there, home of my soul on earth,
Be you,
Be in me – true,
So that I know that you care,
That you're there
And you bear
The thrill of the memory,
The sacredness of the knowledge
That I exist in this world!

Nuart (Nvard Chalikyan)

The Truthful Mirror

"You look strange; you don't look like others",
All the mirrors around her would say
"Your nose is crooked,"
"You are too tall"
"You don't fit, don't fit here at all",
The mirrors bullied the little girl,
And she almost believed in that disgrace
For she saw the world through their lens –
And without them
She could not even see her own face.

But there in the attic,
Among the dust of oblivion
Her grandmother's age-old mirror lay;
It would remind her
Of timeless truths
And of who she really were.
"You are a princess", – the mirror told her,
As she approached him with tearful eyes,
"You are a beauty, a rare beauty" – the mirror said
"This is your true face, with no disguise".
She liked the way she looked in him,
And her face lit up with a smile,
But it was still hard to believe,
For they were too many and he was just one…

She didn't know then,
She couldn't suspect
That all the mirrors around her
Were but crooked and fake,
They reflected the life
Through false lenses,
They were meant for faceless faces,
They took reality to pieces
They showed wolves in sheep's fleeces
And they gained control

Nuart (Nvard Chalikyan)

They showed wolves in sheep's fleeces...
And they gained control
Over shapes and forms, colors and tints,
Over thoughts and deeds...
They told her which roads to walk,
They told her how to talk,
They folded her and molded her
Into something that she was not...
And thus she got used to the kingdom of lies
Where the truth is a challenge, an outcast...

But at the end of the day simple was the deal –
If the girl would believe in the truthful mirror
(the one for whom she was truly dear)
Then the false reflections would all disappear...
For the truth reflected in her beautiful eyes
Could trump the whole card-house of lies.

Your Name

I have engraved your name
On the wings of my soul
So that if I am millions of breaths
And thousands of light-years
Away from this body of mine,
If I ever go through Dante's darkened lands,
Through complete oblivion of what I have ever been,
If I am whitewashed in some unknown fields
In silence and lack of gravity
And stripped of the memory
of this earthly life...
Somewhere there,
Where they can read holy inscriptions
They will know the name of my home...

My soul has your name engraved on its wings
Like a child with his home address in his jacket,
Like a speechless dog with a collar tag.

Shelley Getten

Nature Boy

Even as a baby
you insisted
on being outside,
lulled by walks
in the front pack carrier –
eyes to sky and treetops,
your bobble-head rocking
gently to your dad's
stride as if already
studying the anatomy of trees –
leaf shape of various species,
and beyond them,
the vastness of the Universe.

Mia Loweree

Galactic Star Child

Galactic star child
come back to me,
It seems I've lost you.

Help me Understand again
the things I cannot see,
I miss the mystery and awe.
I miss the beauty & connection..
Once again, I'm striving
for perfection.

Show me again, the perfect
in imperfect.
Show me again, the messages
through nature.

Guide me to the people with whom I can exchange
this Love & Light –
If not an exchange, give
me what I can then give.

I look at the starry night sky,
the seeming ceiling of our Universe,
and I know there's something
there that's beyond my comprehension…

Come back into me
Galactic star child,
I await you –
When I am ready,
I am here,
I am Mia

Sleep

It's time for my body to lay down,
nighttime travel begins…

Where will I go tonight?
Who will I meet?

The adventure awaits –
Many places, many scenes…

Sometimes I do things in nighttime travel
that never happen after sleep ends.

What is the message? I ask.
Will I know when I awake,
that which comes not in words?

What Is the message tonight? –
Delivered through my nighttime travel
I seek to Understand…

It's Raining Leaves

I stand there, leashes in hand,
loves of my life on the other ends,
the feeling of the wind on my skin.

My favorite time of day approaches,
as I see the canopy of the beautiful tree.
Wind blows…..

It's raining leaves,
as the Sun glitters on the fluttering leaf pedals,
Equinox, soon turn back clocks, Fall is here.
Evolve, evolve…
I observe my involvement in the evolvement…

I am there – in the midst of it all,
multidimensional NOW…

1st floor, going up!
There's room for one more, or maybe four..
Do we even need the elevator?
I didn't think so…

Can you feel me?
I feel you from right here,
on the other side of the world.

Sharon Meixsell

Beyond and Before Time and Space

Expanded thought
My two hemispheres joined
Creating new patterns of Love
Creating waves of movement
Extensions of me everywhere
I am multiplied in the Beyond
An endless sparkle of Pink radiance
Angelic beauty in stillness
A heart opening of compassion
Wings of a dove fly towards the sky
I am this Dove full of Peace
Surrendering my Will to the Divine
I am Source wonderment
I am vivid, dynamic waves of color
Flowing, merging, morphing
Into the All of Divine Oneness
I have let my old life go
So that I may grow and expand
In this place/space of me and Beyond
Beyond where two become One
Beyond Time and Space
Beyond that
To arrive at the Gateway of the Ancients
To arrive at the Gateway of the Galactic Beings
Yet, Before that to a place with no name
A place where a new Universe
Is brought into existence
Suns, Galaxies, Planets all are born
The Creation of the Highest Order
Creation of the Cosmos
A Creation that you and I

Sharon Meixsell

Can learn how to co-create
We are the Master Builders
We are the makers of the Multi-Verse

Inside the Sun

Meditating with folded hands
Eyes closed; Darkened room
Sounds experienced through my inner eye
Taking me on a journey in a purple starry Galaxy
Golden Sun with indigo ring not hot too for me
I am allowed to move closer
Only to see it change color, it becomes green
Morphing into the shape of a heart
Spinning vortex of my dreams
It changes to purple; So many rings around it
I move closer and reach out my hand
It moves inside and I see it covered in a gel like fluid
The purple heart beats; I feel the pulsations
My own heart beat moves in sync
A slow melodious sound so deliciously Divine
There are no words I am it and it is me
Whispers of the Spheres all around me
Secrets of the Galaxy laid open
No words; I am awe-stricken
The Heart morphs now into a circle; It has encased me
I am in a bubble of gel fluid protected from all harm
Aquamarine and magenta colors shift and change around me
It is Glorious! My arms open wide I receive this gift
With honor and love; I feel the love oh so much love!
My bubble turns pink as my heart grows bigger and bigger

Sharon Meixsell

I watch as it leaves my body and yet I am still alive
It beats outside of me; It is so beautiful!!
Tears fall silently; There are no words
It moves through the bubble and is shining,
Covered in Aquamarine light
I feel it, my eyes open wide, I take a breath
I become peaceful and serene, I am calm as I feel this all
Yet I have no words for this experience
My hands folded in front of me
I bow to the Sun; I honor my experience
My heart floats back to me entering the bubble
It slides into my body; I am One again
And yet even bigger than before
I now glow brightly as the bubble moves out of the Sun
Feeling so light I am back in the space
Of the purple starry Galaxy
I whisper Thank You; It is all I can manage to say
As the tears still fall and I feel the pull; the tug
Of moving back into my physical body
I lie there for a long time not moving, not thinking
Just on a blank page, a place of no words
I send love to the All and fall into a deep peaceful sleep

Sharon Meixsell

A Drop in the Ocean of Space

Whooshing; Goose bumps on flesh
Purple and lavender streaks
Form like ribbons in the sky
I am a drop in the ocean of Space
A whip like strand of DNA
Spinning a circle of sparks
This is who I AM; This series of colors
This energy you see before you
I am here in the stillness of my Heart
These vibrations raise over my arms
They move and dive into my Soul
I am a child once again; wanting to get lost
Wanting to hide away until
The All that is serious leaves
My Heart dives down deep again
Finds the strawberry Lepiodiolite
And the Cinnabar Diamond
My heart centers as does my Merkaba
Building blocks in the center
Waves flow from my hands; moves others away
So that I may move in sync
As the whip like strands come closer
The sparks of yellow are near
They meld into another color
Crystal clear Diamond Platinum rays
Shifting and changing encircling me
Spinning faster and faster can't see anything
Whip like movements, move out into more space
Feeling myself widen my DNA reshapes itself
I break apart and merge together
I gently come into my body,
Encased in pink and green the vortex subsides
I am One with my Human body

Paul Richmond

Stanley Was Waving

My aunt Sophie
Was born in Poland
She remembers one day
Walking home with her mother
They did this walk daily
Always passing the neighbor's farm
Stanley was usually in his garden waving

On this particular day
She remembers as they approached
Her mother grabbed her hand
And started pulling her
As if to rush by the farm

She was resisting
For she loved to stop
Stanley would usually share
Something from his garden
She loved his peaches

Her mother kept pulling her
Faster and faster
She remembers being confused
Waving to Stanley
As they passed by
Stanley waving back

When they got to their house
She noticed her mother
Was sweating
Frightened

Paul Richmond

Fumbling with the keys
Couldn't get the key in the door

After they were in the house
The doors locked
She asked her mother
Why didn't they stop
Her mother said
Stanley died yesterday

She Already Knew

My mother was in the basement
Doing laundry
As she was putting laundry
Into the washing machine
The basement suddenly felt very cold
She felt the coldness behind her
She then felt a weight
As if a body was pressing against her
The weight of this body
Pressed her up against the washing machine
She felt unable to move
She struggled
She finally broke free
In a cold sweat
Feeling weak in the knees
She crawled up the stairs
To our apartment
Closed the door
And locked it

Paul Richmond

A few moments later
There was a knock at the door
My mother stood looking at the door
Then she heard
The woman from upstairs

On opening the door
The woman explained
Her husband just died
She wanted to let my mother know

My mother
Already knew

I Have Some Questions

I arrived in Belgium
For a juggling convention
I had a book of translations
Of the language I thought
Was spoken in Belgium

As I walked down a street
Checking menus with the book
None of the words matched
Thinking that it was jet lag
I decided
I would go into
The first restaurant I saw

Paul Richmond

As I entered the restaurant
I was met by
A force
So ominous
I was pushed across the street
Bewildered
I stood looking at the restaurant
I asked
Where do you want me to go?

There was a restaurant
A few buildings down

I walked in
Everything went fine
Ordered food without complication
As I sat eating
I noticed an older woman
A few tables over
Talking to the waitress
Something about her
Kept drawing me to look over

The waitress left
I was finished eating
I asked
So why was I to come here

The woman
Looked over to me
She spoke to me
In several different languages
Finally saying something to me in English

Paul Richmond

I found myself sitting at her table
I don't remember getting up
She said to me
You understand this is nothing sexual
I nodded
She said
I have some questions for you

Patricia Dixon

Referents

The words on the page
seek to call up
what is not there –
Images and ideas,
oddments and ideologies,
ripples and referents
to things housed in
the mind's eye.
Memories, music, and movie magic
Stir genius and the imagination to
Meandering journeys, bending
time, folding space, crossing
galaxies, Motara nebulae,
and outracing asteroids,
populating other planets
with weird people who are,
nonetheless, human in their
various ways.
Words -- referents to things –
known, and unknown –
always sought; never caught.

Patricia Dixon

Unsung Melodies of Sisterhood

Why do old women die squirming in remorse
for all the sacred joys lost to a haunted heart-felt peace?
Every thought lingering and devouring dark ghosts
lest they wear holes in a seeping secret memory
where their girlhood poetry danced unseen and unexplored?
So, you born now, eat of our vast bleeding bones
and pierce the ice-cold present with wild nights and easy laughter
putting our silent pains to use
like bringing a magic flower of freedom to those
who weep tears of despair and know it not.
For our lost poetry must be revealed
and brought to light or you will suffer our fate
and die as we die settling for much less
than that of which you are capable.
So, turn your brilliant gaze inward
and find all those hidden places,
all those lost dreams,
all those lost poems
and spread them out in a blazing carpet of passion
for all to see.
So that your daughters,
and their daughters,
and their daughter's daughters,
will have the strength that we lack.

Patricia Dixon

Dreams of a Poet

I dropped off to sleep and dreamed until noon
Of running aloft with the nighttime moon
I dreamed of whales and mystical dark sails
that whispered of midnight and salt ocean gales
The moon sang sweetly as I ran along
Moon-dark trails echoing its melancholy song
She sang a darkly melodious tune
that kept my heart full, but washed me in gloom
I paused in a silence deep and profound
spellbound, enthralled by that mystical sound
I cannot recall, it faded too soon;
but my soul remembers with each new moon

Brian Smith

The Quaint Angel

Her face was haloed by a bright light
that hung above Heaven's gate.

She had the countenance of a Botticelli angel.
Her porcelain skin was smooth like alabaster.

God had spared her the encumbrance of wings,
In favor of long fingers and a thin neck.

She is called "The Quiet One,"
for she chooses to speak in whispers.

She is the white child,
the child of large brown eyes and the quaint smile.

> The child is fair,
> her feet are soft and light.
>
> You would believe
> that she walks on air.
>
> You would believe
> she's been given flight.

Brian Smith

In the Gaps

In the gaps,
the spaces between lines,

filled with thoughts and wonderings,
just fillers for a time.

Spreading spackle
in the cracks,

one way of keeping
the water out.

Holding hands,
or arms wrapped around her waist,

just filling the gaps between us,
giving love one last taste.

Palacios, TX and the Universe

Aphrodite enters the water, lovely as moonlight
screams at her consort, "Leave me alone!"

He's my husband she apologizes
to a sky of cotton candy on cerulean blue.
The water ripples carnival lights.

There's more to know here
a triple threat
space, time, possibility,
sand, water, breeze
and a call from an old comrade.

Luther's cedars have seen it all.
Roaring 20s
the kind of music they play in horror films
before things get weird.

Midnight Cowboy, Blue Velvet, Blue Valentine
3 poets laugh at the nekkid narration
watch that ax; it's mating season

procreation, creation with words
we stand witness to the past
in this vast space of sky and stars,
the edge of the Milky Way,
the big dipper and
another glass of wine.

Sussan Summers

Edge of Madness

The edges blacken
to tunnel vision
then a white light strikes open
the earth at my feet.
I stare into an abyss.
The ground crumbles beneath me.
I step back, slip,
arms pinwheeling
to the growl of flames
and high-pitched shrieks.
I jerk my chin up,
while still skittering backward
atop an avalanche
of dirt and stones,
and find a patch of steady blue
among roiling clouds.
I set my focus,
gather strength,
force two steps back,
fall,
and scrabble backward.
The earth steadies,
my jagged breathing slows.
regain my feet,
back away with a final look
to memorize these coordinates
for the place where madness reigns.

Susan Summers

Seeing Infinity

Focus not on the forest
or the trees,
look for the small animals
beneath the leaf litter:
snakes, toads, turtles.
Look closer,
snails, beetles, worms,
and microscopic
amoeba, bacteria –
transforming rot into resources,
creating vital nutrients for life.
The lowliest comprise the base
where they digest, recycle.

Observe everything at this lowly level;
find the atoms and split them,
transforming matter into energy –

Travel beyond our atmosphere
to planets with their rings, moons, storms
to stars: giants, dwarfs, dying, birthing,
to the edge of the Milky Way,
to Andromeda,
events hundreds of years away –
billions of other galaxies
created by our searching,
we see infinity.

Susan Summers

Illusion of Time

We put time in round cages
with tick tock locks
to pretend we control
the hour and the day.
No stock in our futures;
we cannot bank today.
We spend too much time
thinking things of yesterday.

When everything is Googled,
there's nothing left to say.
We call each other wrong
and quickly turn away.

Ephemeral to infinity,
time flows like living rivers
upon the cosmic sea
and the reflection in the mirror
is not you – it's me,
both of us waiting on the outcome
of things yet to be.

Effervescent as a bubbling spring,
Time's an illusion
to track our progress –
footprints made in air.
We pretend we are here
when we are really there –
beyond imagined galaxies.
The very act of searching
creates something new to see.

We are not many
only one great spirit race
who lives among the stars
in the boundlessness of space.

Susan Summers

A Poet's Box of Time

You have that poet smile and special
sense of knowing
that we are only here a while
and then we must be going
to spread the seeds of poetry
and water wilted gardens
in these times of drought.
You take the negatives
and turn them inside out.
Pump up the positive energy,
remove the doubt.

What can be done
in love and fun
is free expression and good will
and you continue gathering,
never standing still.
Your box of time is filled with memories
and souvenirs to treasure
it has gardens growing
and auras glowing
when we gather all together.
It has some storms but mostly
pleasant weather.

This time of yours cycles back within itself
like the Ouroboros
yet creation exceeds destruction
as desire exceeds the need
so that hourglass sands

Susan Summers

float like snow globe duff
drifting, floating
reversing the time polarization
so we always have enough
of everything we need.
All energies are positive
every poem a seed.

String Theory

works like this:
a husky sneezes in Minnesota,
a butterfly dips in flight
in Botswana.
In Singapore,
a boa lessens
its constrictions just enough
and a black pig escapes
for tonight it's safe.

In New York city
on a deserted pier
a 19 year-old girl
(we will not slander her here)
looks at brackish water
sees a star
and realizes that star is her
for tonight, ah, for tonight
she is safe.

In Minnesota
the same husky sneezes
again.

The Impossible Logic of Time

I stubbed my toe
hurrying to get the phone,
I cursed and limped over to it.
Turns out it was my podiatrist's nurse
who wanted to know
how I was doing.
I wanted to say
"Fine until you called"
but shortened it to say
"Fine"
"Good. Good" she said
and clicked off.
It was just another day of impossibilities.
I heard the neighbors oak scream
as the chain saw approached.
I heard the spirit that lives in my kitchen
ask "What's for breakfast?"
The phone rang again.
I spilled my coffee and slipped in its puddle
and fell to the floor- as I lay there moaning
The answer machine picked up
"This is 911 were you about to call?"

It was that kind of day
filled with anticipation
and unlikelihood.

Mike Gullickson

Time Traveler: For My Son

What I should have said, when I had the chance
is that I miss you, I love you
I want you back in my life.

What I should have said, when I had the chance
is that the river of time is speeding up for me
it is hopeless to resist
its headlong rush to the sea.
No one among us can.

What I should have said if there were a machine
that could change the flow of time
I would turn the power on, adjust the dials
send myself back to when
things started to go wrong
someway, somehow make them right.

I believe we all feel that way.

I would correct all of my mistakes
unhurt those I have hurt
be wise enough and brave enough to say
what I feel in a gentle way
understanding, too well, the power of words.

We both know such a machine does not exist
time can heal or destroy
it is up to us to decide the path it takes.

When I had the chance I should have said
these things
I hope that saying them now is not too late
the bridge we stand on is sturdy
my hand reaches to you.

The Excellent Now

What your mind
will bring you
one day
as you sit on a hill
and watch sacred existence unfolding:
A cloud, shaped like a comma
separates phrases in the sky,
something flies by,
with wings you wish you had,
something brave moves in the grass
towards you. Is it a new beginning?

If you had not stopped on this hill today.
If you had chosen to remain inside
afraid to be involved
you, and the world
would have been poorer for it.

Nothing more important than this:
sitting on a hillside
where you nourish
each other.

Visions, Dreams

In my first vision quest
I went 3 days without food or water
in the Nevada desert.
I stumbled a lot
which was
a perfect description
of my life,
in fact I became an expert at the pitch and roll
walking as if I could not trust the Earth.
Always stumbling, never falling.

On my second vision quest
I climbed a mountain while I fasted
3 days and nights, I walked on scree and bear scat.
I embraced the mountain when I needed to,
which is what I learned: embrace what is in front of you.

My 3rd vision quest was in the piney woods
I learned from mosquitoes the tiniest things can drive you mad.
Which is much like life, constant biting and swatting.
I ran from this quest before two days were through.

My last vision quest?
I will take just after my last breath.
What obstacles will you put before me
as I follow you, Mr Death?

Marsh Muirhead

The World Spins

Hang on! The world is spinning
faster and faster – that orange eye
popping over the horizon just after night
has gone clomping through the house
and out the back door, too late
for coffee – evening already
rolling up at our knees, missing the news –
earth setting a new lap record around the sun,
yellow leaves falling, a turkey in the oven,
the Christmas tree up, down, ice off the lake,
the infrared and the other rays igniting tulips,
pushing up cornstalks, ripening apples
while pages fly off the calendar into space –
golden retrievers, lightning bolts, castles,
twelve shirtless firemen littering the universe.
One foot on the floor is not enough –
grab the bedpost! Close your eyes!

Marsh Muirhead

Flight Delay

Neither God nor the airline care,
or were ever responsible, for the
long awaited getaway with your secretary,
or your mother's funeral, the trip
to Disneyworld, five years in the planning,

the ticket, only a provisional contract, your idea,
weather, jet engines, a rested crew permitting
to get you, perhaps yours, from A to B,
maybe on to C with your luggage which,
as we know, often goes to Bemidji, not Bimini.

You lie on the cold three a.m. floor
clutching your carry on, your pillow, sleepless
under an airport blanket so thin it provides
less comfort than nothing, inspiring only despair
beneath the fluorescent lights and maddening

announcements telling you what you already
know: that the best laid secretaries
and dead parents, the lovers and travelers,
the families strewn about concourse H,
often go astray.

Marsh Muirhead

The Missing

The dental records do not match,
and so
this person is not the missing person,
although
this person too is surely missing
from somewhere,
missed by someone
for about the same length of time
as the missing person we know.
But since this one is a stranger,
she will be folded away
and forgotten,
missed by no one we know,
as far as we know,
for now,
taking her place
in the waiting room of the news,
unable to find a chair.

Marsh Muirhead

Memory Care

The brochure advertises *catered living* –
hot meals and linen service,
medication management,
double rooms for the spoused,
pull cords and grab bars for everyone,
bingo, billiards, and a spa.

Forget icy sidewalks, trips to the pharmacy,
cabin fever, the cabin itself,
even the car – almost everything
can be forgotten in one of the
memory care neighborhoods –
Idyllwild and Bel Aire,
Blueberry Hill and Strawberry Fields –
everyone's comfort and security forever.

The invitation is illustrated
with notions of careful dancing,
someone reading by the fireplace,
a silver-haired gentleman
poised at the edge of a pool,
a game of cards,
and there! – a candlelit supper
and someone pouring wine,
no one, it seems, suffering any pain,
not even the blues.

Marsh Muirhead

Haiku

October moon
everything
on this side or the other

three a.m.
the call that doesn't come
fills the house

I can't see you now
she says
meaning *ever*

longest night of the year
no answer
for the owl

last week of school
history
slows to a crawl

last night of the carnival
the tilt-a-whirl
whirling empty

a thousand snows
again
the pasqueflower

A. Marie Kaluza

Wrong Train

Whirligigs as remedies,
things spin without thought of stop.
Twisters take long strolls down Westlake Avenue,
heavy and drunk with the morning news.

People reap without sowing,
kill without drawing blood; I talk to a man
at the metro station and he says his legs were blown off
by a computer 10,000 miles away.

Shadows as memories,
we shake hands and drink to that.
We pull our hats down low and pretend,
shake off the dust that has covered everything.

I ride the rail until I don't see anything;
bodies come and go, landscapes blend and ripple.
The train slips inside me, electric wire weaved
into my thick, bulging veins.

I am too tired to note the encapsulation of my life.
It's only when someone else
hits the brakes, I take notice that I hopped
the wrong
train.

A. Marie Kaluza

A Bedridden Lullaby

I am sinking swift as a canoe yearning for its belly to flop skywards
and drown itself in Easter pill piles and linen bandages and hour
second waits, aching for a bit taste of capillary crunching eat
and acrobatic feats like strolling and sitting and sleeping
through the night without my stiff mother coming in
and pestering me if I'd be alright *Be you alright,
child?* So sometimes I would pretend I'd be
out like a doorknob and dumb to all the
trembling of the trees letting go of
all their ashen leaves and quiet
like a shrew into winter I'd
go shine myself up as a
dime to roll my body
away into a dream
where nothing
here is the
same.
Then,
like a fine
dandelion kept
dead for too long
I burst slowly fragile
and clanking as if every
bone had forgot how to be a
bone how to be working late and
such so they need a good dusting like
shelves buried neath paper stacks for eons,
but, things are moving faster now as if I am in a
hurry to be a human being, grinning myself into fast
catch up and scarfing and runningrunningrunning papa
say *Oh my word you be a tiger!* going beyond what you came
from and starving your lungs while whipping like a wild beetle in
springtime heat; and I got all the mouth to howl at the horizon all the
damn much that I want to howl at it everything tastes like being alfresco.

A. Marie Kaluza

Upon Some Other Shore

Next to me is a pillow with a hole I cannot fill.
The chill of Memory empties her cup.

It never comes. The fruit rots before the ripening.
The darkness arrives before the dawn and light.

You were never here. You never slept beside me.
As a shade, you couldn't have died.

And you don't die. Every morn you rise with me.
I hear your laugh echo, feel your leg shift under mine.

I clutch my fists and curse bitter endings.
I rake my arms across my desk and scatter objects.

I break hearts and bones. I'm bedeviled by lies.
When will I stop clinging, to your ghost?

Every hour, I toe the line.
Every hour, you respond in kind:

All this brooding is unbecoming of you.
I am sorry, for the wreckage, but you will be alright.

I burn these candles down to their nubs.
I look at your white shoes by the doorway.

All I do is wait and wait, for the last drop to be squeezed out.
For the last scent of you, to at last leave the house.

Leave and find roots upon some other shore.

A. Marie Kaluza

Slow
That which does not kill us, must have missed us – Miowara Tomokata

At the sound of a word
my hair frails and thins,
my skull is held whole with pins,
I'm filled with foreign liquid and life
spills onto a bedsheet.

I clutch at the air. I twist,
tire and lie down upon my grave's lap.
This is the game: the tug and push and roll.

How slow can I make the world go?
A strong throw of a stone into deep water;

How long shall it remain within sight?
How long before a thing recedes into time's depth?
How long before a yellow leaf
detaches and dries?

I have options. I have possibilities.
Things aren't over. Things don't end,
not really not really.

I am carved out some more.
I fade into the dark,
barely visible barely visible;
I still use my fair share of air.

People tell me a watched pot never boils.
So I watch myself pale.
I watch myself grow spots.
I watch my legs, give way beneath me.

A. Marie Kaluza

I watch the papers get signed.
I watch the drugs go into my mouth.
I drag on   and on   and on.
The happening
always just around the corner.

Charles Darnell

Gray Running

The morning is clear.
The track shines with sun's rays
reflected off cinders.
Stretching gets the kinks out
and warms stringy muscles.

A slow jog for a mile or so,
listening to the crunch
beneath your shoes,
a rhythmic cadence, quickening
as you fall into routine.

You run by yourself,
preferring the lone monitoring
of body movement,
of breath, of sweat beading,
dripping off the tips of fingers.

No, the speed is missing,
though the heart calls.
Old legs move more slowly,
lungs do not hold the air
as in younger days.

Yet the feeling's the same,
determination winning out,
to strive and take joy
in the struggle,
and life in the pain.

June Blumenson

Voodoo in Cartagena

I hadn't bargained for the shacks
along the tarmac at the airport,
or the air pressing like a death mask
when we deplaned.

The black sky transfixed me,
and the evening, searching for the moon,
held its breath in chilling stillness,
as if warning all to stay away.

I had a strange dream that thick night:
a child lay close beside me
and when I woke, the heat
from the child's body slipped away.

It was then I heard the drumming
of the surf, could almost touch the intrigue,
saw myself running into the opaque
sky, wild like someone gone mad.

Was it stories I'd heard of kidnappings
and bandits in the hills, voodoo
dolls for sale and talk of black magic
rituals deep in the jungles?

Was it drug cartels, armed guerrillas
or that tall, swarthy man hitting
on me as I sat in the outdoor cafe late
into the night drinking scotch and water?

Or was it the baggage I'd brought
with me to the impossible
beach-all riled up like a desert storm?

June Blumenson

Memoir

I crumple the hard copy,
hit delete, and gone
are the missteps, the proof
of failure, as if it were possible
to preserve the journey or throw
it away; as if a memory card
inside us could permanently record
our lies, sustain happiness,
withstand sorrow,
and like a black box
someday explain everything.

There are some important
things to know about a black
box: it's not black,
it's international orange, how
much more fitting, metaphoric,
considering the times when lost,
we need to send up flares.

The black box immortalizes
two hours of history,
recording over and over itself
in a loop, beaconing
up to thirty days to signal location.
Imagine that – our last hours
of conversation, our voices
pulsating beneath the ocean,
yet incapable,
one last time of calling home.

June Blumenson

A Dog's Life

Instantly, he jumped up to nestle
his head against her neck –
(forgetting his noble lineage)
rolled over and sat on her feet
so happy he was to see his mistress
from a past lifetime
in another perfect human rebirth.

At first she did not know him
but when they looked into each other's eyes,
greetings of ten thousand souls
reverberated between them.
So tender was her scratch behind his ears,
so softly she said, *ah, my loyal friend.*
He heard the longing in her voice,
the rasp of time, the wear
of too many dog years of despair.

What had happened to them over all the years?

All he knew was that not one lifetime
went by that he did not think of her,
wonder what sign she would give him,
how he would know her,
so he could show her his love again.

June Blumenson

You Don't Have to Be a House to be Haunted

or breathe the stagnant air of abandoned
places where beasts go bump
in the night and you wake to eat the cold.

You have only to witness the thumps
in your chest, old haunts scented
with rosemary, the lemon poppy seed cake
you still taste as though it were yesterday.

You don't have to be a house to be haunted,
you have only to receive the sun's
radiant burst upon your shoulder,
or your dead mother's arms that embrace
you when you sit in her chair.

The people you once loved run over
your skin. They stretch and grin inside you,
crack you open, reveal a scythe of moon.

June Blumenson

Ancestral Dream

She'd come undone, sprung out of a wall cloud, her hair dripping tornados. And she squeezed and squeezed until all the weather drained into the farmhouse tub that was sinking into the rotten floorboards where a violin was hidden beneath worn linoleum tile. "Don't," I shouted to this phantasmagoria (who looked like me) when she brandished a knife as if she knew what she was doing and started to pry the tile up in bits and pieces. I heard the dry stretched, catgut strings snap – the metal wound so tight on that old fake Stradivarius, and my grandfather sat up in his grave – stared into the white night – the music in his belly weeping; he was still afraid, even in death, that the Czar's army would catch him running away to Brazil.

June Blumenson

Stuff of Wounds

If I were an alchemist,
I would conjure
rubies from the flame,
change dust into magic
powders, teach time to stay,
transform the world
into a place where trees
never lose their leaves,
and dreams
do not have wings.

The stuff of wounds
would turn to silk,
every broken promise
would find repair,
and all the bitter
on our tongues
would melt into elixir,
sweet and full as golden
peaches in summer,
and the bones we pick
from ashes
would be made whole.

Christine Beck

Given Salt, Given Time

　　I.
Before I knew that olives grew in Spain,
and bloomed on ancient trees, their
accent on the tongue a foreign zest –
Kalamátas, Arbequiñas, Manzañillas –

Before I knew that olives should grow full,
turn black or purple-brown on branches first,
then cure in brine for weeks in wooden casks,
their bitter taste stripped out by salt and time,

I thought black olives came in cans called Ripe,
displayed on crystal plates in Large or Jumbo size.
I didn't know they'd been picked green, then dunked
in lye and gassed to turn them black and firm.

　　II.
Before I knew what burrowed in her skin
would claim my mother's life at fifty-two,
leach out exuberance, her sass and flair,
strip hair from blonde to driftwood gray,

we holidayed in Spain, slipped into bars,
bought local wine, a meal with cheese and bread.
Aceitunas, olives, were required to turn
the commonplace to the sublime.

We feasted on their oily olive skins,
a soft resistance, ooze against the tooth.
We flicked our tongues against each fingertip,
licked the dripping oils, and sighed.

III.
That was before I knew what I know now,
that olives on the branch, grown full and lush,
will lose their clutch. They fall into the nets
below, still bitter and inedible.

Yet soaked in brine and stored in casks,
given salt and given time, the olives will turn
plump and savory as memory, a picnic
on a small Majorcan beach.

I Am Writing to You from the End of the World

The hunger artist, hovering outside the carnival tent,
casts an empty eye on a possum decomposing.

A sculptor rips the bronze off screeching wrens,
swallows, hawks, as they tear holes of havoc in the skies.

Two lovers stare at laundry as it sits in graying suds.
A woman nearby smelling of righteousness

and newsprint stares down a man whose red tattoo
says "I don't trust anyone."

A pickup truck drives by, Jesus
painted on its side.

Christine Beck

Time Sensitive Material

Time etches lines around my lips, the ones
I pressed against the scented envelopes I sent
that summer you were in Peru and I was on the Cape.

Time lurches through the years, bursts
like fireworks, spreading sparks of royal blue,
stark against the sky.

My letters moved from desk to desk each time
you changed your office, sealed in a cardboard box,
brought home when you retired.

When I opened it, the letters burst to life,
my words of ever after, written
to a man who never read them.

Einstein had it right:
Time is its own dimension,
refusing rules of logic or chronology,

an endless loop of then and now, what happened
and what never could, endless loops of royal ink
etched on a sky blue envelope.

Christine Beck

Rewind

When she rewinds the plot,
plays it through the centuries

Mary wonders what the thirty years
were for, for

Jesus could have shown up
fully formed, like Adam

God knew how to make a man, make
a human, give him choice

She wonders what the thirty years
were for, for surely Jesus didn't

need to practice as a carpenter,
study Torah for the rules.

Why the thirty years? Unless,
perhaps they weren't about the son,

for him to fall in love with life, to
feel the wood smooth under fingers.

Perhaps the plan was diabolic: to
give her thirty years to fall in love with

him. Why would God desire to make
a woman suffer more than needed

for the sacrifice? She rewinds the
story, tries to see the moment

Christine Beck

when love turned into dread, when
she began to see the final scene,

began to see the master plan.
Unless, of course, the sacrifice

was not his life, but hers. The one
left keening, the one left just alive.

Becky Liestman

Grand Mound: A Sacred Prehistoric Site on the Rainy River

Alone, a little girl, astonished
turns to the frozen soil
rich in spirits, pottery and artifacts.

Long silent, the Laurel tribes
came to this forest, this water
to fish sturgeon, gather ripe blueberries.

They came to bury their dead.
Listening to her heartbeat she hears them
speak of wind and natural things.

Her body stands calmly in the melting snow,
surrounded by last year's tall grasses.
Her soul is open.

She turns to peer into Canada.
The river runs between nations.
Sap flows freely from sugar maple trees.

The ancient ones join her.
Today they are river mist in moist spring air.

They send her a vision –
birchbark canoes in foggy twilight.
An eagle calls upriver.

Becky Liestman

Kay, One More Time

Loyalty hung round her like reeds in her hair
like webs and frailties of root bound beliefs
like sea weeds and the captured sun of windowsills.

In the hot cool afternoons sheltered from the winds
that buffer our barrier island
she sat motionless, except for the small flame
hitting the ashtray, rising to cut potatoes
for the deep fryer. Smiling.
An Irish rebel, she wore cardigans.
I have one. Even so, I never started smoking.

Bobby, was a commercial fisherman
he hung by the wharf and brought in giant blue fin tuna
winched up over trash cans and gutted with chain saws.
He had a world record, almost, but the Japanese
swung it onto a factory boat and cut it to bits before they yelled
out the weight – 1200 pounds.

Who cares.
Kay worked for groceries fishing being peculiar.
An old, young mother, she sat on our island, just past the sand dunes
her kitchen table her always place. Welcome I joined
had a diet coke. I was 23, she was old then, probably 32.
She knew some stuff about life I was trying to get.

Sometimes, we walked the beach off-season
the wind hitting hard, the Atlantic our brilliant
difficult bedfellow.

Sometimes we ate at the clam shack, winds
slowed by the heat of flat calm days, the tuna in, basking.
Like the story of waves
there isn't any end…

Meditation

She stretches her fingers wide
imagining a day among days –
skipping stones near Duluth harbor;
black rocks catch the morning mist.
They crunch underfoot.
She can still hear that sound.
She holds her day in her hands,
her whole world, gazes at it,
picks at some tiny lint as she once
picked scales from newly-caught fish.
Bright pictures appear.
She brings them into focus,
elongating her time tunnel.
She sees herself. She barely hears
the quiet slap of waves,
a bicycle bell in the distance.
She practices looking. The lens
of her eye peers inward, mesmerized.
Her questions still, her skin softly folds.
She waits. She sits.

Becky Liestman

My First Pocket

I peer into myself,
a private eye to the keyhole –
I am child,
motion caught
by tarnished jeans.

As I watch, I fiddle.

In my third pocket –
spent wishes
morning hope
and my father.

I hum
drawing them together,

with a thread I string a fantasy bead a full circle of myself.

Patiently work to blend the whole
eye at the keyhole
for comfort.

At a knot
I wonder,

Where does my father, the breath of centuries
in his cool heart,

belong?

Becky Liestman

Hear Me

I rise from the sea of myth.
Find me at the bar on Water Street
shuffling with wannabe fisherman.
Inhabit it. Live it like your lover.
Aim toward miscalculation,
polar division, deep ports and swell sprays.
You'll need shadows, clues, a seaworthy sextant –

maybe a shifty slant, a twitchy eye?
I'll be here, sounding myself together
in hope. Come.
Ring the dinner bell. Scan the damp menu.
Track dusty prints under the broken bar stool.
Play hangman in the back lot by the boat docks.
Fill in every letter.

You'll see me in the vagaries of the mist
catching a blue wave on a night crest.
You'll see me at the jukebox playing
Black Lion Blues, a song that isn't there.
I'll be drinking tap beer, my last dollar waterlogged,
wilting. You'll find me on a bar stool, swaying.
You'll help me sing my swan song,
the one I call Escape.

Becky Liestman

She Did Not Hear

She *saw* the sounds
as if her body lifted
swelling on the waves of their melodies.
She became more than white light
more than fogged moonbeams out her window.

She rose on the banks
of high notes and swam in the hollows
of descending scales.

The sounds were everything.
More than smoke in rising air, more than nimbus clouds,
they guided her.
She opened to the beats of her life;
she held her singing heart.

Becky Liestman

Specimens Like Us

Lit by dawn and sheared by sundown
Pinned to the landscape,
We are past proud.

Set on a billowing Minnesota field,
Almost as if
We'd perched on hay bales indefinitely
Watching Amazing Grace drift by
Out in that blue sky –
Forever.

No, our lifetime's less telling,
The only story we keep.

Passing bees float in lazy loops,
Mimicking the liquid light-dark circle
Of days, a lazy lasso
Covering us.

Pulling us gently, solemnly
Toward that spiral of distant life,
Wheeling us onward to what we may have been.

Becky Liestman

China 1013 A.D.

Again and again, people unwrap,
        unwind, violate the treasures lovingly placed

to honor ancestor spirits in ancient graves.
        Come, pry open the past –

It is one thousand years ago. It rains.
        A wet breeze moistens the grasses,

while ancient men without souls – determined –
        shovel, break the clay on a moonless night, sweat.

Loot gold rarities and jewels. Jade burial vessels –
        symbols of purity, nobility – fall apart when they drop.

Plundered treasure overfills dirty sacks while heated village dogs yelp,
        inflamed. Villagers race to graves on strong skinny legs,

brandish sharp poles, too late, their ancestral tombs are ruined
        empty, fresh with digging and despair.

The ancestors rise up, mouths open to be appeased,
        bitter, hungry ghosts left desolate as the robbers' escape.

The peasants' duty no longer conceivable, their tears are endless,
        they turn together to the south – wailing.

One thousand years later, a lone girl appears, tangles her fingers
        in the same tall grass, the rain gentle.

Before and after, is night and daylight.

Becky Liestman

Hey, I Say

We've been sheltering since morning
under cover of light

on a small rise
in a half breeze.

A train comes and goes
with its long sounds.   Distant.

Can you believe our luck?

There she is,
the white fawn,

making her bed
like a lamb in the scrub.

Her mother keeps the secret

watches
unaware by the dry creek.

We blend into the
landscape.

A hawk rises. A grass bends.

Everything is simply
one moment.

Becky Liestman

On My Doorstep, I Expect a Miracle
Town Lake, Austin TX

it's so *dry now*
trees across the river make a show
their leaves a cluster of orange, red
yellow

the river stretches steel blues
and iron grays,
rippled muscle

sculling boats clunk by
oars supported by outriggers

the boats feel distant –
like that long ago river too dry to float
buffalo hides out to sea

strangers in cranes
transplant live oaks, old majesty
I rise in sympathy, dust
whirls by

it's December – I walk the green grass
muscovy duck in my path
the cormorants are gathering
a blue canoe tied to the red dock waits

Dr. Charles A. Stone

In the Creases

Days fold into days
then are crumpled into weeks
…months …years …eternities;

Somewhere in the creases
I lost you… found you…
lost you again.

Only a thread of your love
remains… stitched into
my dreams,

But when winter winds
wrap around my ashes
I will split the seams of time

As I search every corner
of the universe
for a trace of you.

Dr. Charles A. Stone

The Easy Bridge

The rest of this illusion
may vanish with time
but the easy bridge
between us, the one
built on foundations
of red earth and
suspended by
moonbeams
will outlast
starlight

our spirits
will forever
dance in the
wild embrace
of trees breathing
the fresh air of spring
storms while the grey
sea turns blue and all
around us morning turns
our night into another day

Spheres of Reality

your spirit and mine are encapsulated
within our personal spheres of reality
spheres that interact with one another
in seemingly brownian fashion
though their intersecting courses
are hardly random explorations
of time or space or in between

within the sphere of your reality lies
intelligence tempered by compassion
insight softened by tolerance
and curiosity turned to confidence

within the sphere of my reality lies
anticipation among other things
that each sphere, like a soap bubble
blowing in the wind, will burst
in the course of time
and reveal within it
your every secret

in the course
of time

Medicine Wheel

Born under the Moon of the Strong Sun
I see through glasses of carnelian agate,
respond to the beating of my heart
and am steadfast in love.

Born under the Moon of Earth Renewal
you see things through eyes of crystal quartz
and transmit the energy of the universe
to those you embrace.

I am Flicker, whose incessant drumming
is calling you to a nest lined by feathers
singed venetian red by flying
too close to the sun.

You are Snow Goose, soaring above frozen lands
on wings of the North Wind with precise and
graceful swoops in flocks that inspire
earth-bound spirits far below.

I am Frog clan and you are Turtle clan,
yet the Medicine Wheel says we are compatible.
I know this – we are the twining
of wild rose around the trunks of birch trees,
the *tick* and *tock* of passing time.

Dr. Charles A. Stone

Chance Encounter

each wrong turn leaves a scar
on the stippled lining of my psyche

so when I turn around abruptly and
knock the avocado from your hands

I stutter an apology and try to explain
about wrong turns and scars

while a blemish creeps across
the surface of the peach I am holding

but wrong turns are not all random events
you say as you survey the produce in my basket

our meeting here might yield fruit of unknown sweetness
you whisper between the lines of your own apology

then you explain how each wrong turn leaves a bruise
on the plum-smooth surface of your psyche

we blush strawberry red when we realize
how much we are alike

you ask how many wrong turns I think
might have led us to that aisle

I ask how often we might have crossed paths
and not been aware of it

we each wonder how many scars and bruises
we have accumulated during the years

that preceded our coincidental meeting
among cherries and pears and jalapeno peppers

then we turn and go our separate ways
with our blemished fruit and wounded psyches

still I sometimes wonder how many wrong turns
we each have made since that chance encounter

Unfamiliar Form

Chance encounters may not be chance;
they may change strangers in undisclosed ways
or they may remain inconsequential thrums
in the background of genes and protoplasm.

Perhaps a power in outer space controls
the encounters, much as stars might cause
snow to fall, as the moon controls tides
and tides dictate the shape of beaches.

Most chance encounters are unseen, silent
but if your body changes to sand, to spirit
and then to another preordained or unintended
form after we part, how will I recognize you?

Parallel Lives

It is not a chance encounter,
the two of us   sitting next to one another
at a counter piled eye-high with expectations,
you asking me to please pass the cream,
my eyes   savoring your croissants.

I believe someone is playing with us
and we are willing players in the game –
perching like blue jays on our stools,
introducing ourselves with a flourish of napkins,
rearranging silverware   in kama sutra positions.

I am not surprised when you offer to share
your two-for-the-price-of-one croissants
and you are nonplussed when I sip
your ice-water and pick up the checks,
before helping you into your parka.

We are strangers who aren't strangers –
I know which was your car without asking,
you know that I am Virgo,
have a birthmark   high on my left thigh and
trace it on the back of my gloved hand while I skate

into your glacial blue eyes
as I have on so many other occasions,
etching my name on the smooth surface
of your psyche, a reminder that I am
your evening star   in a parallel universe.

Dr. Charles A. Stone

Everywhere the Stars

I may have lived one life

with you

in the time before we met

or were born,

in the time we watched

clocks

in the eternal blaze beyond

the stars.

I'll never know the whole of it

or understand

how time spirals around the truth

of our love.

I can't remember the future

or forget

what it was like before we met

last night.

Was it just last night or was it

a lifetime ago

when we passed one another

in the market

but continued our separate ways,

eyes averted,

like poles of a magnet searching

opposite directions,

knowing that we would not

meet again

under these skies until one of us

or both

had coins for eyes and whispered

through earth?

Publication and Other Credits

Christine Beck
Given Salt, Given Time ... in *Blinding Light* (Grayson Books, 2013)
Rewind... in *Blinding Light* (Grayson Books, 2013)
I Am Writing to You from the End of the World...in *Stirred, Not Shaken* (Five Oaks Pres, 2016)

Claire Vogel Camargo
Riverstone Words... in *PST Yearbook: A Book of the Year*, 2013 and *Poetry at Round Top Anthology*, 2015

Barbara Crooker
Equinox... in *Radiance* (Word Press, 2005)
This Poem... in *Line Dance* (Word Press, 2008)
Irrational Numbers... in *Radiance* (Word Press, 2005)
At the Last Chance Saloon... in *Small Rain* (Purple Flag Press, 2014)
Sometimes, I Am Startled Out of Myself...in *Radiance* (Word Press, 2005)
Phases... in *Triplopia,* 2006

Joyce Gullickson
For Clarity's Sake... in *Another Rescue Attempt*, 2014; *Earth Day Contest*, 2015; and *The Love Anthology*, 2015
A Tribute to Our Favorite Spot... in *Di-Verse-City*, 2013; and *Another Rescue Attempt*, 2014

Hemmingplay
The Tunes of Life... *Hemmingplay.com; spillwords.com; mytrendingstories.com*
North of Tombstone, 3.a.m... *Hemmingplay.com; Wildsound Writing , Toronto* (text and video); *Poetry Breakfast (poetrybreakfast.com); Allpoetry.com*
All Is Temporary... *Spillwords.com*
Breathe Briefly... *Spillwords.com; Mytrendingstories.com*

Angela Hunt
Email from a Small Star... in *My Father in Verse: Writing Through the End of Life*
Surprising, Isn't it... in *I Am Still Me: Brains Are Injured, Hearts Are Mended* and *Concerning War: A Collection of Recollections with Room for Rumination*
We're Doing Swimmingly, Thank You... *Chaska Herald*, 2012

Glynn Monroe Irby
Jump-Fly... in *3 Savanna Blue* (Plain View Press, 2000)
Phosphor Nights... **in** *3 Savanna Blue* (Plain View Press, 2000)
The Swan-Goose... in *3 Savanna Blue* (Plain View Press, 2000)

A. Marie Kaluza
Upon some Other Shore... Poet's Corner, 2016

Becky Liestman
China 1013 A.D... version in *Di-Verse-City*, 2013
On My Doorstep, I expect a Miracle... in *Texas Poetry Calendar*, 2010
Grand Mound: A Sacred Prehistoric Site on the Rainy River... in *Blue Hole*, 2016 and version in *Where Rivers Converge*, 2016
I Open My Life... *St. Louis Park MN – Artist of the Month*, 2012
Hey, I Say... in *Preoccupied with Austin* as Watching and Waiting, 2012 and version in *Texas Poetry Calendar*, 2012
Kay, One More Time... *Inks Lake Ink*, 2007 and *Di-Verse-City*, 2006
Specimens Like Us... in *Poet Artist Collaboration* and a version in *Di-Verse-City*, 2006

John Looker
Raiding The Deep... in *The Human Hive* (Bennison Books, 2015)
Bottom Remembers Love... in *The Wagon Magazine*
Frequent Flyers... in *The Human Hive* (Bennison Books, 2015)
In the Time of Eldorado... in *Shimmering Horizons* (to be published)
First Landfall in Nova Scotia... in *Shimmering Horizons* (to be published)

Mia Loweree
It's Raining Leaves... *Divinely Inspired* (mialoweree.com, 2016)

Aimee Mackovic
Purple Vesper... Erasure source: Pareles, J. "Prince, an artist who defied genres, is dead at 57." *New York Times*, 2016
1984... Erasure source: Palmer, R. "The year's best: 1984 in review." *New York Times*, 1984

Neil Meili
Rule Britannica... in *Putting Aside the Mask for the Moment*, 2016
Dante's 9th Inning Stretch... in *Putting Aside the Mask for the Moment*. 2016

John Milkereit
If We Lived at Sarah Oppenheimer *D-17*... in *Di-Verse-City*, 2013
Before I Start Reading This... in D*i-Verse-City*, 2011
Enter My Honeycombed Vault...in *Di-Verse-City*, 2016
Disclaimers on Reading... in D*i-Verse-City*, 2007

Marsh Muirhead
Flight Delay... in *New Mexico Poetry Review*, 2009
The Missing... published as "The News" in *Frogpond*, 2015
Haiku (titles are first lines) –
October moon... *Modern Haiku*, 2012
three a.m. ... *Modern Haiku*, 2011
I can't see you now... *Modern Haik*, 2009
longest night of the year... *Key West Citizen*, 2008
last week of school... *Modern Haiku*, 2010
last night of the carnival... *bottle rockets*, 2013

a thousand snows... M*odern Haiku*, 2016

Nicola, James
The Wrong Place... in *Stage to Play* (Word Poetry, 2016)
Traces... in *Loch Raven Review*, 2011
Have You Ever Woken... in *Rattle*, 2016

Nuart (Nvard Chalikyan)
The Mystery of the Universe... *Di-Verse-City*, 2016

Brian Smith
The Quaint Angel... in *Where Rivers Converge*, 2016

Pat Smith
Unpacking for the trip... in *Blue Hole*, 2016

Dr. Charles A. Stone
Chance Encounter... based on poem of same title in *Di-Verse-City,* 2003

Biographical Sketches

Christine Beck holds an MFA in Creative Writing from Southern Connecticut State University and is the author of *Blinding Light* (Grayson Books 2013), *I'm Dating Myself,* (Dancing Girl Press 2015),and a chapbook, *Stirred, Not Shaken* (Five Oaks Press 2016). She teaches poetry, creative writing and literature at The University of Hartford, Southern Connecticut State University and in private workshops, directs a monthly series at the Hartford Public Library, and produces a monthly community television show called Poetry Around the Town. in which she interviews poets and poetry activists. She is also a board member of Riverwood Poetry Series and is a former president of the Connecticut Poetry Society. She was named the fifth Poet Laureate of West Hartford, 2015-2017. www.ChristineBeck.net.

June Blumenson has returned to her love of poetry after a career in human services as a psychodramatist, group therapist, and administrator. She is a member of The Loft Literary Center, Minnesota Poetry Therapy Network, teaches poetry classes, and curates a poetry reading series. Her work has appeared in many literary journals including Adana Literary Review, Boston Literary Magazine, Comstock Review, Earth's Daughters, The French Literary Review, Literal Latte, San Pedro River Review, and the anthology 'Times They Were A-Changing: Women Remember the '60s & 70's.' She was a finalist for Nimrod's 2012 Pablo Neruda Prize for Poetry, and in 2014 won the Loft/MIA Sacred Shorts Writing Contest. Her poem, *Dogs of War*, inspired by the sculpture Some/One by Do-Hu Suh, was posted at the Minneapolis Institute of Art near the sculpture. June's poetry collection *Swallowing the Mountain* is currently looking for a home.

Lynn Wheeler-Brandstetter was born in Canada, resides in Texas and spends her spare time with her family, writing poetry and mentoring students in Hutto, Texas. She is CFO of a family owned, small entrepreneurial business and for over a decade has served on the Board Of Directors for Austin Poets International. She has been writing poetry based on life experiences from a young age.

Claire Vogel Camargo discovered her poetry muse later in life. Her poems have recently appeared in San Pedro River Review, Texas Poetry Calendar, Best Austin Poetry, Enigmatist, Blue Hole, Di-Verse-City, Snapdragon: A Journal of Art & Healing, Deep Water Literary Journal (Ireland), Illya's Honey, and various haiku publications: Haiku Presence (UK), World Haiku Review (UK), Brass Bell, Cattails, Failed Haiku, Lifting the Sky: Southwestern Haiku & Haiga, and in her chapbook *Iris Opening*. She is on the Austin Poetry Society Board of Directors, is a Writers League of Texas member, and holds Bachelor & Master of Science Degrees in Nursing.

Barbara Crooker is the author of eight books of poetry, including *Les Fauves* (C&R Press, 2017) and *The Book of Kells* (Cascade Books, forthcoming). *Radiance*, her first book, won the 2005 Word Press First Book Award and was finalist for the 2006 Paterson Poetry Prize; *Line Dance,* her second book, won the 2009 Paterson Award for Excellence in Literature. She has received the 2004 WB

Yeats Society of New York Award, the 2003 Thomas Merton Poetry of the Sacred Award, and three Pennsylvania Council on the Arts Creative Writing Fellowships. Her work appears in a variety of literary journals and anthologies, including Common Wealth: Contemporary Poets on Pennsylvania and The Bedford Introduction to Literature. She has been a fellow at the Virginia Center for the Creative Arts seventeen times since 1990, plus a residency at the Moulin à Nef, Auvillar, France and two residencies at The Tyrone Guthrie Centre, Annaghmakerrig, Ireland. Garrison Keillor has read thirty-one of her poems on The Writer's Almanac, and she has read her poetry all over the country, from Portland, Oregon to Portland, Maine, including The Calvin Conference of Faith and Writing, The Austin International Poetry Festival, Glory Days: A Bruce Springsteen Symposium, and the Library of Congress.

Charles Darnell lives in San Antonio, Texas. He is a member of the Sun Poets Society and is a regular at the Society's weekly open-mic. His work has appeared in anthologies, magazines, and journals including Voices Along the River, Di-Verse-City, Right Hand Pointing, Still Crazy, The Enigmatist, and Blue Hole. He is past winner of the Tempie-Skerritt Poetry Prize and the San Antonio Poetry Fair Award. He won the "On Fire" poetry competition in Bangalore, India in 2013.

Patricia Dixon holds a BS in Occupational Therapy from LSUMC-SAHP, New Orleand and a MA in Professional Writing from UHCL, Houston, TX. She is working on publication of her next book, *Extenuating Circumstances*, an experimental work of short fiction and poetry which should be available in Spring of 2017.

Shelley Getten is a poet and visual artist. She works full time as a special education Paraprofessional. Her poetry was most recently published in Migrations, An anthology of transitions, Talking Stick, and Spillway. She received a residency at the Anderson Center in Red Wing, MN, and an Honorable Mention award in the 1999 Rainer Maria Rilke International Poetry Competition. Her chapbook, *Agates*, received a second printing from Finishing Line Press in 2015. Shelley lives and works in Minnesota on the North Shore of Lake Superior.

Joyce Gullickson is a registered nurse and poet. Her poems promote peace and hope, "waking people up" and re-establishing connections with each other. A collection of poetry, *Another Rescue Attempt,* is available from Amazon. She has been published in The Map Of Austin, Di-Verse-City, Sunscripts, San Antonio Hot!, Via Poetry on the Move, and The Enigmatist, which she co-edits. She is co-host of the Georgetown Poetry Festival, which publishes the chapbook Blue Hole.

Mike Gullickson was born in Milwaukee, Wisconsin. He publishes two magazines, The Enigmatist and Blue Hole. He has read on NPR and had a poem on the game show Card Sharks. He has over 100 published poems, in the U.S. And England.. as well as 4 chapbooks and a book of poems called *A Promise of Music.*

Jonathan Harrington lives in an 18th century hacienda in rural Yucatán, México where he writes and translates poetry. He was an invited reader at the International Poetry Festival in Havana, Cuba. A graduate of the Iowa Writers' Workshop, he has published five chapbooks of poems. His translations of Mayan poetry have appeared in numerous magazines as well as a full-length translation of Feliciano Sánchez Chan, published by New Native Press. In addition to poetry, he has published a collection of short stories, authored a collection of essays and has published five novels.

Hemmingplay has been writing fiction and poetry around the edges of his life, but took a slight 46-year detour to work as a reporter and editor in newspapers and in higher education public relations among other things. He states that writing poetry is a kind of retraining program. It requires finding the nugget of truth in things, and describing it in a few well-chosen words. This is a skill that will come in handy in the novel he's working on.

Angela Hunt holds a degree in the Psychology of Communication from Concordia University and is a Minnesota State Certified Librarian. She was an assistant buyer for a major Minneapolis department store, and wrote radio monologues and plays on weekends. Two radio programs, *Scripture in Song* and *Building Blocks*, ran for several years on KNOF-FM. She is a librarian whose service to the community includes Adult Story Hours for the developmentally challenged and brain injury survivors, as well as Memory Care Story Hours for Alzheimer's patients. Her books of poetry include *My Father in Verse: Working Through the End of Life (*translated into German); *Am I Still Me?: Way Out on a Limb: A Mother's Journey Through Her Daughter's Rape*; *I Am Still Me! Brains are Injured, Hearts are Mended*; and the upcoming *Concerning War: A Collection of Recollections with Room for Rumination*. She appears in the first Carver County Anthology, Where Rivers Converge, won first place in the Arts Consortium of Carver County Poetry Contest 2016, was posted Poem of the Week on the National PenWomen Society website in 2016, and earned a spot in Crossings of Zumbrota Poetry-Art Contest and anthology in 2016.

Glynn Monroe Irby is a graphic designer and co-author of the book *3 Savanna Blue*, and the cover designer or editor for over 40 books of various other writers and publications. As a poet, Irby has been published in the Houston Poetry Festival anthology, Di-Verse-City, the Southern Poetry Anthology, Borderlands Texas Poetry Review, San Pedro River Review, Sol Magazine, and others. He is a member of the Galveston Poets' Roundtable, an Honorary Lifetime Member of the Gulf Coast Poets, and was selected in 2006 as one of the "Bards of the Bayou." For several decades, Irby was the manager and designer in a furniture and design business and is a Retired Professional Member of the American Society of Interior Designers.

Gilbert Juergens III Gilbert is a Scandinavian-born poet whose identity and work has been uncovered recently during a search of family archives. He is a collateral relative of William Riley, a poet whose first publication was in Preoccupied with Austin, the 20th anniversary anthology for AIPF. Gilbert has read poetry at several local venues in his adopted country and is working on his first book of poetry.

Becky Liestman is a poet and fiction writer. She received a residency at The Writer's Room in Greenwich Village in NYC and was nominated for a Pushcart Prize. She was a winner in both the Austin International Poetry Festival, and the juried Poet Artist Collaboration at the Crossings at Carnegie. She was also awarded a juried residency at Cummington Community for the Arts in Massachusetts. Her poems have appeared in poetry journals and anthologies including Preoccupied with Austin, The Texas Poetry Calendar, The Enigmatist, Blue Hole, Talking Stick, many editions of di-Verse-City, Lifting The Sky, Where Rivers Converge, Soundings East, and Main Channel Voices. She is published in Crosstimbers, a journal of The University of Sciences and Arts in Oklahoma. She has 2 poetry chapbooks, and is working on a third. She loves to spend time with writers, leads fiction and poetry workshops, and lives in Minnesota.

John Looker lives with his wife in southern England. His home is a small town close to the intersection of the historic Pilgrims Way to Canterbury and the track of an ancient Roman Road from London to the coast. His poetry has been taken into the UK national collection at the Poetry Library and been published in The Wagon, a literary journal in India, and online at Poetry Breakfast and elsewhere and has been read on local radio. In his book *The Human Hive*, John Looker explores our common humanity, down the ages and round the globe, by looking through the lens of work and human activity.

Mia Loweree was born in 1965 in Florida and has been writing poetry since elementary school. She has explored many occupations since obtaining her GED after she left home at age 16. She carries a certification in Permaculture, as well as Akashic Record Consulting. She is a poet, writer, artist, and lover of nature, the Universes, the metaphysical and Spiritual, & recognizes her connectivity to everything physical & non-physical. She lives in Dripping Springs, Texas with her 2 loving canine kids and is a dedicated Akashic Record Consultant & Universal Intuitive Practitioner.

Aimee Mackovic earned her BA from Wake Forest University and her MFA in Poetry from Spalding University. Her chapbook, *A Sentenced Woman*, was published by Finishing Line Press. She has two other self-published chapbooks, *Potpourri* and *Dearly Beloved: the Prince Poems*. Her work has appeared in Main Street Rag, and The Cresset, among many others. She has been awarded residencies at the Millay Colony and Breadloaf Writer's Conference. She is currently professor of English at Austin Community College. Please visit aimeemackovic.com for contact information.

Neil Meili is a long-time AIPF poetry attendee, past director and featured reader. A Canadian in love with Austin, Texas, and author of more than thirty collections of verse; including such classics as *My Uncle Shot My Dog*, and *Take Two Haiku And Call Me In The Morning*, and most recently *Putting Aside The Mask For The Moment*. Website NeilMeili.com.

Sharon Meixsell lives in Washington State. She is a Soul Poet and a Multi-Dimensional Channeler who writes Spiritually Conscious poetry and channels Cosmic Energies passing on messages to Humanity to help raise their vibrations as they awaken to Higher Consciousness. Her poetic messages include topics such as: Self Love, Sacred Union, and One with the All That Is. In July 2016 Sharon published her first solo work, *Loving My Self ~ A Journey of Transformation"*, as an audiobook with Raven Audio Books. In May 2016 Sharon's poetry was in the 7th Annual Isis Women's Arts Festival. You may find more information on her website, http://www.sharonthesoulpoet.com.

John Milkereit is a rotating equipment engineer working at an engineering contracting firm in Houston, TX. His poems have appeared in various literary journals such as Texas Poetry Calendar and San Pedro River Review. His chapbooks are *Home & Away* and *Paying Admissions* (Pudding House Press, 2010). He recently completed a low-residency M.F.A. program in Creative Writing at the Rainier Writing Workshop in Tacoma, WA. His new collection of poems, *A Rotating Equipment Engineer is Never Finished*, was published March 2015 (Ink Brush Press).

Jeffrey Morgan is the author of *Crying Shame* (BlazeVOX [Books], 2011). More recently, his poems appear in Copper Nickle, The Kenyon Review Online, Ninth Letter, Poetry Northwest, Rattle, Verse Daily, and West Branch. He can sometimes be found at thinnimbus.tumblr.com.

Marsh Muirhead is a semi-retired dentist, commercial pilot and flight instructor, and former bodybuilder (Mr. Minnesota 1983 -- although evidence of this is now scarce) who lives and writes on the banks of the Mississippi River in northern Minnesota. His fiction and poetry have been published in Rattle, Southern Poetry Review, Flint Hills Review, Water~Stone Review, Carolina Quarterly, and elsewhere. He is the author of *Key West Explained - a guide for the traveler*, and a collection of haiku, *Her Cold Martini*.

James B. Nicola has had poems appear in the Antioch, Southwest and Atlanta Reviews, Rattle, and Poetry East. His nonfiction book, *Playing the Audience*, won a Choice award. His two poetry collections, published by Word Poetry, are *Manhattan Plaza* (2014) and *Stage to Page: Poems from the Theater* (2016). He won a Dana Literary Award, a People's Choice Magazine award (from Storyteller) and a Willow Review award; was nominated twice for a Pushcart Prize and once for a Rhysling Award; and was featured poet at New Formalist. Lately, he has been giving both theater and poetry workshops at libraries, literary festivals, schools, and community centers all over the country. A Yale graduate, James is also a stage director, composer, lyricist, and playwright; his children's musical *Chimes: A Christmas Vaudeville* premiered in Fairbanks, Alaska. sites.google.com/site/jamesbnicola.

Nuart (Nvard Chalikyan) lives in two worlds – the horizontal and the vertical. In the horizontal world she lives in Armenia – an ancient country with a warm heart.

She did her first major in English language. Later, she specialized in International Relations (Cambridge University) and currently works as an international relations specialist, and as a journalist. In the vertical world, she inhabits the magical world which gives birth to poetry, music, art and other unexplainable things that talk to the soul. She has been writing poetry since she was a schoolgirl but has only started publishing recently. Her poem *Mystery of the Universe* was published in Di-Verse-City 2016.

David M. Orchard is a professional geologist with degrees in anthropology from Stanford University and geology from the University of Texas at Austin. His poetry reflects his life-long fascination with those subjects, coupled with enduring admiration of great literature. His poems have appeared in Cenizo Journal, Di-Vêrsé-City, A Book of the Year 2013, Texas Poetry Calendar 2017, and Map, a publication of the Geological Society of London. He is at home in Houston, Texas and Ukiah, California.

Jim Parker is a lover of language, literature, life, laughter, and learning. He traveled south from Michigan many years ago to become a transplanted Texan and to find his true calling as a teacher at St. Francis Middle School. He is the editor of El Lobo, the literary magazine at St. Francis School. He also worked as co-editor for the Di-Verse-City Youth Anthology in 2014 and 2015.

Georg Reilly was born in a small town 150 miles from *anywhere* to parents of Euro-Caucasian lineage. He has been engaged in epistemological debate for too many years to count, and is publishing here the first of his poetry on the time-space continuum. A product of a Jesuit education, he prefers the obscurity of his own place in the universe to that of the limelight, but in time will resurface to test the boundaries of life as a published poet. He has authored one chapbook: *Under Other Guises*.

Paul Richmond has been an artist and performer for over 40 years. He created Human Error Publishing, which organizes monthly readings and annual Word events/festivals, (Greenfield Annual Word Festival) and publishes independent writers. He has published four books; *No Guarantees – Adjust and Continue, Ready or Not - Living in the Break Down Lane; Too Much of a Good Thing - In the land of Scarcity - Breeds Contempt*; and *You Might Need A Bigger Hammer*. His fifth book due out 2017. Paul has been published in numerous journals, anthologies and has been a featured poet throughout the country. www.humanerrorpublishing.com.

Brian Smith lives in the Twin Cities western suburbs, and is a lifelong resident of Minnesota. *The Art of Confusion* is his first published work of poetry. His writing focuses on giving the reader a personal look at this crazy and wonderful world we all live in. His intent is to share thoughts and ideas that readers may find interesting and enlightening.

Patricia Young Smith holds a Ph.D. in English from the University of Minnesota. She taught writing and literature at several universities, including the

University of Kentucky, where she also became the managing editor of an economics research journal. After retiring, she began writing poetry as well as continuing to write articles and longer pieces. She has a poetry chapbook, *Sparkles and Sand*. She's been published in Wind, Blue Hole, and other publications. She has ghost-written memoirs for high-achieving professionals, and won a poetry prize at the Carnegie library.

Dr. Charles A. Stone was born in Green Bay, Wisconsin. He earned doctoral degrees from Marquette University and Johns Hopkins University under his given name. During his academic career he authored numerous scientific articles and edited several medical textbooks. His poetry has appeared in regional poetry journals and anthologies; he is also responsible for several chapbooks, 9 books of poetry, three works of non-fiction, and two poetry anthologies. He is currently on the Board of Directors for the Austin International Poetry Festival.

Susan Beall Summers is an over-educated, under-achiever who has traveled from the swamplands of South Georgia to the Pyramids of Egypt. She interviews poets for Texas Nafas, Channel Austin, is a member of Writer's League of Texas, Austin Poetry Society, and Gulf Coast Poets. Publishing credits include Ilya's Honey, Texas Poetry Calendar, Harbinger Asylum, Yellow Chair Review, Di-Verse-City, Cattails, and Frog Pond. She has a full length collection and a recent chapbook. She has given feature performances across the country and remains unapologetic about her open mic addiction.

Joyce Sutphen grew up on a farm in Stearns County, Minnesota. Her first collection of poems, *Straight Out of View*, won the Barnard New Women Poets Prize; *Coming Back to the Body* was a finalist for a Minnesota Book Award, and *Naming the Stars* won a Minnesota Book Award in Poetry. In 2005, Red Dragonfly Press published *Fourteen Sonnets* in a letterpress edition. She is one of the co-editors of *To Sing Along the Way*, an award-winning anthology of Minnesota women poets. Her fourth collection, *First Words*, was published in 2010; in 2012, *House of Possibility*, a letter press edition of poems, was published by Accordion Press, followed by *After Words*, which was published in 2013, and *Modern Love & Other Myths* (2015), which is a finalist for a Minnesota Book Award. She is the second Minnesota Poet Laureate, succeeding Robert Bly, and she teaches literature and creative writing at Gustavus Adolphus College in St. Peter, Minnesota.

Michele Vecchitto is a wife, mother, and middle school teacher. Her work can be found on Stepstimestwo.wordpress.com. She continues to hone her craft simply to breathe life into the stories living in the corners of her mind. She has written a blog for two e-commerce sites, as well as completing works of poetry, and novels.

Roger West is a poet, songwriter, performer, punk rocker long before and long after it was fashionable. He was born in London, England but now spends most of his time in SW France, writing, recording and performing in French and English, influenced by those 'liquid stories' that ebb and flow across the Mediterranean and wash up on its shores. He is part of the Urgence Poésie collective, is on the

Board of the Austin International Poetry Festival, has published four books of poems and contributed to a French anthology of *'poésie de la marche'*. He has read and performed at Austin International Poetry Festivals, and at festivals in France, Morocco and the UK. His current place of residence is Gignac, France.

Disclaimer. In light of conflicting standards for citing publishing sources, the editors have opted to use italics for cited poems, chapbooks, collections or books of poetry by contributing poets. Other books, journals, anthologies, magazines, newspapers, websites and other such sources appear in standard font; this, we feel, is the best way to highlight the poets' work.

Made in the USA
San Bernardino, CA
07 January 2017